Acknowledgements

I would like to dedicate this book to my late mother Mrs Patricia Ward. My mum was a wonderful person, strong, independent, and very family orientated. She passed these characteristics onto her siblings, or her girls, as we were known. My mum gave me strength, integrity, determination and courage to live my life and pursue my dreams. She taught me that sometimes you have to fight for what you want, what you believe in, and what you stand for. She showed these strengths whilst she was ill with the dreaded cancer. Nothing phased her. She grew mentally stronger and stronger on a daily basis and her will to live become more cemented. Unfortunately, the cancer was stronger than she was. And in 2005, she was taken from us. My mum was only 59. This is no age to die. Seeing this made me realise, just how short life can be, but also how glorious moments can change your life forever, however small.

Fulfil your dreams today as tomorrow may never come.

Chapter One

Well here we go again. The weekend is here. I'm a 37-year-old woman, living on my own. Well not quite on my own, my daughter is now 17 years old and quite truly a young lady in herself. Bringing her up was never an easy task. Single parenthood can be very difficult. But to be honest I think that if I had a man around (especially her father) during this time, I would have probably killed him. Men, you love to hate them, yet you love to love them.

It's Friday night and I have had an exhausting day at work. I want to party and I want to party hard! I know, I sound like a teenager!! But I missed out on this little devilish experience, of drinking like it's going out of fashion and then coming home at 7am in the morning, after a night of hard-core dancing.

It sounds funny to me that a 34-year-old woman would want to carry on like that. What the hell I need some fun. Did I say 34? Hmm. No I do believe that I am 37. Hold on; let me do the maths. Had my daughter at age and ah yes she is 17 that makes me 37. How ridiculous. I cannot even remember my age. Giggling away to herself, she sits on the sofa. I am a high powered executive and cannot even remember how old I am! How funny.

How rude of me. My name is Elizabeth or Lizzy for short and I am a single mother of one. I live in the wonderful town they call Walthamstow. Can you hear the sarcasm? Only jesting. I have a typical 2 up and two down, with a garden you can just about swing a cat around. And oh yes ALL of the neighbours can see me. I must do something about that. I keep meaning to. Every year, I prance around in my bikini in the garden, and every year the neighbours ogle me. There are 2 strains of thought on that one. They are either thinking, look at the state of that, and has she no shame! Or simply admiring my beauty. I like to think it is the latter, to be honest. And anyway, I don't' care what they think. Hmm. Yes I must get some Dimmock activity going on in that garden. Not today though. It's Friday night and I want to party.

She looks at the clock and realises that it's 8.30pm already. All of her friends have a man, and no arrangements have been made for the weekend. What a bummer. Kiss is blaring in the background and Lizzy has just poured her first glass of Chardonnay. Australian Chardonnay at it's best. Yes Lizzy graduated from the likes of Libframilch and Lambrusco, many years ago. Yuk, just the thought of that turns her stomach. Kisstory is thumping out on the radio. Lizzy is singing at the top of her voice.

"I'm surprised to see your suitcase at the door, de de de de de don't you want some more"! Dancing around like a disco diva!

Feeling totally single and raring to go, she phones her mate, Jenny.

Jenny is the crème de the crème of women. She knows who she is, what she wants and more so, how to have a good time. Lizzy has a lot of respect for Jenny. She is bold and beautiful, intelligent, and funny. Lizzy saw Jenny as a bit of a role model, and was sometimes in awe of her confidence. Nothing seemed to get to Jenny. Whatever life threw at her, she was always bubbly and vivacious and had this cest le vie attitude.

"Hey Jen, what's the plan for tonight?" Lizzy said

"Lizzy, me old ripper! How's it going??"

They both chuckle full heartily.

"Lizzy, I've got a date. I'm so excited. I met him last week at my brothers, mate's house party and he called me. He is taking me out for dinner!" explained Jenny.

Well that's nice, thought Lizzy. Party last

weekend and no invite, and she is supposed to be my mate. Dismiss those thoughts girl. You are feeling bitter and left out, that's all. People move on and times change. Get a grip, she says to herself.

Lizzy has all of a sudden become quite deflated. Kisstory is still playing in the background, but does not seem to stir up the same excitable emotions.

"Liz are you still there!" questioned Jenny.

"Yes hun, no worries. Ok fill me in tomorrow. I want to know all of the details."

Lizzy puts down the phone and redials. This time she speaks with Sam.

"Hey Sam, it's Lizzy. What's happening tonight then?" asked Lizzy

"Liz, how are you? I am going out with the other half. For once he has left his kids with the ex and is taking me out for a night on the razz. His due any minute now".

"OK hun. Catch up soon. Must dash" sighed Lizzy.

Sam was one of Lizzy's closest and oldest friends. Sam was bright, in-fact very bright. She had an exceptional job, a high powered executive in the banking industry, was very well respected in her field and very much the professional career women. Lizzy was truly fond of Sam, however, why she had bothered to ring Sam, she does not know, as it was always the same. You see, Sam has been living with this guy for over four years now and rarely ventured out with her mates. This man, if that's what you can call him, was a nasty piece of work. He prayed on Sam's vulnerability, yet she absolutely adored him. He never, ever seemed to contribute to anything, spent most of his time smoking weed, he never really did anything for her, pretending to be something that he clearly wasn't. Yep he was an arsehole, a sponger, a taker, and he totally took at every opportunity he

4

had. Just the thought of him annoyed Lizzy no end. But there was nothing she could do about it. Sam was totally besotted with him. I hate that man, thinks Lizzy. Sam also knew exactly how Lizzy felt about him. He is such a no hoper. But hey, Lizzy was just feeling jealous as she was single, and deep down whilst she didn't want to be with someone like Sam's guy, at least Sam had someone and Sam has a date and Lizzy don't. Lizzy felt herself feeling rather agitated. He is a waste of space. Lizzy tells herself. In-fact waste of space is too good a phrase for him. Shame Sam does not see that side of him. Perhaps he is good in bed. Yes that must be it. No one in their right mind would put up with that rubbish. Unless, he was hung like a horse and knew exactly where every woman's erogenous zones are. Well talking of every woman, I'm sure he has had plenty! After, the in depth head consultation with herself, Lizzy suddenly feels that she is all right with being single. Even though she has been for the past 4 years, but just of late she has slowly become the only single girl in her circle of friends.

Feeling even more deflated; Lizzy fills up her glass and runs a bath laden with her favourite bubbles Calvin Klein Eternity. Humming away to herself, *'you've got to show me loooove, words are so easy to say......* The song fades into the background as Lizzy soaks in the warm water.

Chardonnay to hand and candles a blazing, she resigns to the fact that she is not going out tonight. This is the second weekend in a row now. Even Shelley has a date! Shelley is a lot younger than Lizzy, by 10 years, and they had known each other for around 8 years. It was a strange relationship, as the age difference didn't seem to matter. Shelley was fun, full of energy, and worked as an accountant in the city. Now, accountants normally have a reputation for being boring and dull, but believe me, this girl was far from it. They had spent many a weekend out on the razz, just plainly having fun, getting drunk, and dancing the night away. One great thing about Shelley and Lizzy friendship was that they always came home together at the end of the night, if you can call 7am the end of the night. They never left each other to go home alone so the other one could go off with a man, however nice he may have appeared. Lizzy respected that immensely. But it's not to say that they didn't go off with men together, as a foursome. No, not that kind of foursome!!! We might be fun time girls, but we are definitely not slack.

The chardonnay and bubble bath had now kicked in nicely and Lizzy was feeling relaxed. And then as if a light bulb had come on in her brain, she has an idea. A strange idea, but a good idea. She had been feeling somewhat sorry for herself and a bit neglected by her fellow girlies, but this light bulb moment idea seems to be the answer. Lizzy is not one for sitting in her house, especially at a weekend. She had done plenty of that, whilst bringing up her daughter alone. Back then it was ok to be at home at the weekend, she was a mother to a small child. It was acceptable. But not now, when her daughter is grown up, and very rarely around anyway. Lizzy needed to be out there, in the social realm of adulthood, having fun, meeting people, meeting men and she is not one to give up that easily. This plan will work and Lizzy is about to spice up her single life, by 100 times! She giggles away to herself at the thought of this plan, like a naughty little school kid.

Chapter Two

Girlie holidays! Have you ever been on one? I mean a full-blown girl power experience. I never experienced this until two years ago. There were six of us. Two I knew well, and three I never. Friends of friends. You know how it goes.

"It's all booked, I can't wait". Says Gina, all excited. "We fly on the 2nd April, sunny Spain here we come. Ha ha. I wonder if we will meet any Senor's. Eh Senor, Hola, Buenos dias". She giggles uncontrollably.

"Gina", Lizzy stops her in her tracks. "Is everyone going? I know Shelley is going. What about your friends. Are they all still up for it?"

"Yes, Lucy, Trish and Gemma have booked. We will meet at yours and go to the airport from there. 6 am. Is that OK?" asks Gina.

"Yes that's cool. Got to go. Speak later" says Lizzy as she puts down the phone and sighs. Hmm. What have I done? I have never been on a girlie holiday before. Nah, should be fun, she tells herself.

Lizzy looks up from her office computer and scans her environment. People are busy working keyboards tapping and phones ringing. And then, there he is. Luke. Luke is the ultimate in men. Her thoughts drift away with her. She sees her and Luke, watching the sunset on the beach in Barbados. Cuddling up together. Still with the ocean breeze blowing softly on her tanned skin. The sunset full of promise and beauty. She leans forward, lips puckering, to tenderly kiss Luke's lovely round, soft lips, whilst caressing his beautiful toned midriff.

"Lizzy, what you doing?" Questions a puzzled Luke. Lizzy comes out of her trance and realises that she has been mimicking her daydream, to her astonishment, Luke is standing next to her.

"Nothing" Lizzy exclaims.

Feeling totally embarrassed she tells Luke of her planned girlie holiday that she is going on next week.

"Girlie holiday, you?" He questions. "I did not think you were into that sort of thing".

"I'm not really, but hey you know me, I'll try anything once", states a blushing Lizzy. Still feeling embarrassed and hoping he did not read her mind. Lizzy decides that it's time for a coffee. Whilst making the coffee she pictures Luke. What a man. 6ft 2", amazing blue eyes, dark hair and a body to die for. A definite catch, but for some reason Lizzy just won't go there! There was definitely a chemistry between them, however, Lizzy already knew that office romances just do not work. *Remember that time with Chris?* She ponders.

Lizzy was working in a printing company at the time and Chris was the production manager. She was fairly new to the industry but had been given the key accounts to manage. It was a fun place to work, very creative and with very down to earth people working there. Chris was 6ft tall, dark brown hair and ever so handsome. He would often come and sit with her on his break and just chat about anything. He had a wonderful temperament and Lizzy enjoyed his company. Lizzy never realised that Chris had the hots for her until, one night a few of the work colleagues went out on the razz. Chris and Lizzy were sitting alone, outside the pub, and Chris leaned in for a full on snog. Lizzy accepted, gracefully. It was soft, gentle and stirred something up inside her. At the time, she put it down to the booze. However, the next minute Chris had decided that they were now an item. Lizzy wasn't sure what to make of it, and initially tried to get out of it, putting it down to the fact they had been drinking. But Chris was very persistent. He wanted to be with Lizzy and she found it quite endearing. So she went along with it. At first, it was great. It was their secret. Any opportunity they got to have a quick snog, in the kitchen, in the factory office, they would do it. It was exciting

8

and passionate. It was just what the doctor ordered for Lizzy's boring life. Or so she thought it was. It was a bit of a whirl wind romance really, yet it actually felt right. It was best kept a secret, in her mind. Those people she worked with loved a gossip and she didn't want to be the topic. This went on for a few months, and then the bomb shell. He wants marriage! Lizzy in her normal style would run a mile. Commitment has never been Lizzy's bag. Although she wanted marriage it frightened the life out of her. But something told her that this could be good. Chris's proposal was not up to much, and it did not go according to his plan. He had thought it all through and had booked a table at the local Italian restaurant. Lizzy did not have a clue, what was about to happen. To try and not to make things obvious he decided to invite Lizzy's daughter to the restaurant, thinking that she would decline. But it backfired and she accepted, therefore no romantic proposal happened. It was a good job really as Lizzy would have been totally embarrassed.

Two bottles of wine later, Chris, Lizzy and her daughter arrive back at the then flat, Lizzy was living in and thought a nightcap of brandy would be a good idea. Lizzy made sure her daughter was sleeping before the two of them descended to the bedroom. They took the night-cap to bed, both of them rather sozzled from the night's alcohol intake. Lizzy put her pyjamas on and got into bed. Chris was hovering and then all of a sudden, out of nowhere, he decides to 'pop' the question.

"Will you marry me?" he said, thrusting a little box into Lizzy's hand. In total shock Lizzy opened the box to see a beautiful solitaire gold diamond ring.

"Oh that's lovely" Lizzy said closed the box and then gave it back to him. *I don't think that went down too well*, Lizzy thought, chuckling to herself at the mere thought of it. However, she did accept his proposal, and was quite into the idea of it. She felt that he would look after her, no matter what. Chris adored Lizzy, and in her mind, that what she needed. Thinking about him bought fond memories. She had really liked Chris, but she was never really in love with him, but more the idea of what he was offering.

Yes Chris. What a lovely man. *Until he stalked me* she thought. Yes you heard me, stalked me! Prior to the stalking, he moved into her home. She wasn't really comfortable with it. Lizzy was used to her own space and she often felt that he was in her way. He followed her around the house and it began to irritate her, and the fondness she felt for him started to dissipate. At work, he would take every opportunity to speak with her, there was never a moment that he wasn't by her side. Their secret had been revealed and he would constantly pester her at her desk. He started complaining that she was too friendly with the male clients, and that she should not speak with them. How could she not speak with them? It was he job. To top it off, a staff meeting was called. To Lizzy's horror, they congratulated her and Chris on the engagement. She had started to feel claustrophobic and had tried to explain her feelings to him on several occasions. He started to wait for her shift to finish so that they could leave together, even though they drove in separate cars and his shift finished 3 hours earlier than hers. It was getting too much for Lizzy. She started to think about the relationship, her feelings, and whether this was the right man for her. She decided to take action and left her job due to Chris's paranoia. It was a huge decision to make considering she had a daughter to support and a home to keep. But she needed to get some space back in her life, a little bit of sanctuary away from him. He did support her until she found her feet again, but drove her insane with his paranoia and jealousy. For three months she suffered while he lost his mind. The doctor gave him Prozac to ease his tension. He would walk around the house humming to himself and it nearly drove Lizzy crazy. This lovely man that adored Lizzy went from being a strong, sensitive, kind and generous man, to a quivering wreck. Was she partly to blame? Lizzy will never know, but I am sure that her reactions to his actions, were partly the cause, and thinking about it Lizzy feels a small sense of sadness. However, leaving the job and putting up with the Prozac moments, was all worthwhile as Lizzy came up smelling of roses when she landed herself a better job than she had previously. The tension had eased slightly between her and Chris as she started to feel like an individual again. Chris seemed happier in himself, but continued with the Prozac.

She had been working in the new job for a month or so, and remembers going home to get ready to meet some of the girls at a pub in Wanstead. She had told Chris about her plans, and he seemed happy. He wasn't home when she had arrived, of which she had found strange and she quickly showered and changed. Her daughter was out with some friends. She jumped into her car and as she pulled out of her turning, there was Chris, in his car. An H reg., Fiat. He had been hiding around the corner behind the bushes, waiting for her to leave the house. He knew she was going out and he knew she was meeting her new work colleagues. Yet, it was now clear that he did not trust her. She had not given him any ammunition to make him feel this way. It was his own insecurities that were rearing their ugly head, and Lizzy was not helping the matter by reassuring him. Whilst the relationship had become more stable, she had found that she was feeling very cold toward him due to his behaviour. She was all out of reassurance. As Lizzy drove away towards the A406, she could see Chris in her Interior mirror. Chris was following her in his car. Lizzy was amazed at how bad things had got and decided to replicate the driving style of Schumaca, thinking that would get rid of him. Laughing away to herself Lizzy lost Chris on the dual carriageway. Why she found it funny she doesn't know, perhaps it was her nerves. But then low and behold, he had caught up. She pulled into a pub car park and was now lost. Chris followed her, jumped out of his car and then started thumping the door of Lizzy's sports car.

"Where are you going, are you meeting your boyfriend?" he screamed.

He had really lost the plot and Lizzy could see hatred in his eyes.

Lizzy reversed the car out of the parking bay and then stopped. Chris stood in front of the car shouting obscenities. She didn't understand what was going on. Why was he behaving this way? What was going through his mind? Just the thought of the hatred in his eyes, makes Lizzy shudder, even today. She had to get away and Lizzy was having none of this. She revved the engine and plunged the car forward, attempting to hit Chris's legs. He moved out of the way and she spun off. She was shaking and frightened, but was more pissed off that she was lost. Eventually she found the pub.

Her girlfriends were already inside and waiting. Lizzy told them what had happened and they thought it was hilarious. Whilst Lizzy laughed along with them, she had a sinking feeling in the pit of her stomach. She was furious but also really quite scared. She ordered a drink from the bar to calm her nerves, all the while trying to pretend that she was ok. The, out of nowhere Chris's face appeared behind the large window of the pub, bopping up and down, trying to find Lizzy, who had now hid behind a pillar by the bar. The girls found this eve funnier, but Lizzy was disturbed by it all. Lizzy's recollection of this account does make her laugh, now, at the time she was petrified. The next day she reported the incident to the police and told them that she had attempted to run him over and the reasons why. She was actually concerned that that he would try and have her arrested. The police officer looked rather bemused by the story, but took the details down anyway.

She knew that she had to get out of the relationship. She didn't go home that night, which probably fuelled Chris's suspicions even more. After the trip to the police station, she made a quick call to her friend, and arranged to stay there for the weekend. Lizzy went home, and Chris was waiting for her. He had been crying and looked a mess. And then she did it, she ended the relationship and requested he move out. He begged and begged for her not to do it. So she offered a compromise. "Ok Chris". Lizzy was calm and determined. "We will still get married, because that's what you want, however, I am letting you know now, that I will be having affairs all through the marriage. Because I can tell you know, that is exactly what is going to happen." Chris was absolutely stunned by what she had told him, and Lizzy knew that he would never agree to that. "No, I didn't think that is what you wanted Chris, but I mean it. Otherwise you have until Sunday to leave my house. I suggest you leave". And with that she walked out of the house. On route to her friends, she felt bad, really bad. What had she done to this man? He was clearly devastated, but she couldn't live like that anymore. Still, she was so glad to be out of that relationship, and has never looked back. But at least now you know why she doesn't entertain work romances.

Coffee in hand Lizzy had completely forgot about her embarrassing moment with Luke and started to think about the holiday. What to take, what not to take, how much money to change to euros. What a worry. *And this is supposed to be fun*?

Chapter 3

Lizzy was not one for routine or even the hum drum of the daily rituals. She was very much a go getter. Although, she was sometimes restricted, by being a mother, she would be out and about at the very first opportunity she got. Don't misunderstand her though. She was very much a doted mother and a good mother. From the time her daughter was borne, at the tender age of teenage hood. She decided then and there that she would not be a stereotypical single mum, living in a council house and signing on the dole. It was the norm for people to think that young girls got pregnant just to get a flat. This was not the case for Lizzy. She had met her first love at 16, moved in with him at 17. They had their own rented flat. She thought that she would live loves young dream. She had her man, she had a good job in the city and then she wanted a family. She had everything that she wanted. At that point she did not know what a complete tosser the father would turn out to be. Beating her at any opportunity he had. Sleeping around and abusing her love. He left her no choice but to bring up her child by herself. She loved him with all of her heart. Well as much as you possibly could at that age. She left him when she was five months pregnant, 1 month after he had kicked her in her stomach and told her that he did not want the baby that they had planned together. It took a lot of guts for Lizzy to leave his sorry arse. She was only 18 and did not have a clue about motherhood. But then who does when it's their first child, regardless of the age. Lizzy new she had more to offer her baby, being a single parent. She also knew that she was going to make something of herself. It was only a matter of time. She was a determined youngster. Although her dreams and aspirations were of the normal kind for someone leaving school, she was determined to fulfil some of it. For years she thought she needed a family unit. Someone to look after her, and her baby. A good strong man around the house to help fulfil that unit. While she waited for this man to magically appear, she continued to look at other ways to enhance her life and decided she needed to be further educated in order for   her and her young baby to have security. For the first 3 years of her daughter's life, she did not do much. She stayed with her daughter and nurtured her. She even tried going back with the father. What a waste of time that was. It never lasted long with Lizzy throwing his clothes and video out of the bedroom window. That was his exit, never to return.

When her daughter was 3 Lizzy enrolled in a course at college. This, Lizzy thought would be the first step to financial freedom. The first step to securing her place in the world and being the person she wanted to be. She had ambition and wanted a career. If she was going to go to work it had to be worth her while, financially and mentally. To hell with men. Although Lizzy said this with venom, she really did want that special someone. As the years went by Lizzy convinced herself she did not need that special someone and threw herself into developing her career and mother hood.

In the last term of college, Lizzy found herself in a relationship. It was not predetermined. She went out clubbing with some friends and he just happened to be there. He was a friend of a friend. He was tall and muscular, with a deep voice. The others called him the Gentle Giant. Lizzy had taken an ecstasy pill that evening. She had never done this before and had not been to a big club before. The music was pumping and the DJ was mixing. The ambience in the club was really nice. Everyone looked happy and people appeared really friendly. The pill had not agreed with Lizzy. All of her friends had taken them and they seemed fine. She wanted to sit down as her legs felt like led. She did not like this feeling. She was frightened. She spoke to Sam, and told her that she wanted to go and find somewhere to sit. Sam beckoned the Gentle Giant to go with Lizzy. Lizzy walked around and finally found a step to sit on. Gentle Giant sat with her and they began talking about everything and nothing and she started to feel better. Gentle Giant gave her a bottle of water and was quite attentive towards Lizzy. For the first time that evening she started to relax. One of the bouncers stopped them in their conversation and told them that they could not sit down. He told them to get up and was aggressive in his tone. She had had enough bad feelings in one night and stood up from the step. She

15

was appalled when Gentle Giant grabbed her backside and pulled her towards him and tried to snog her. Lizzy slapped him around the face and told him not to take liberties. She then stormed back to her friends ranting about what he had done. They were not interested as their pills were in full force and they were out of their heads. What a way to meet someone. She often thought this to herself. However, Lizzy did start a relationship with the Gentle Giant. How this had escalated Lizzy still does not know today. This man treated Lizzy like a queen. He would take the stars out of the sky, if it was possible, and give them to her if she wanted them. He helped her move house and then never left. He was always there. Always there for Lizzy and her daughter. He was a perfect man. He would massage Lizzy every night with essential oils. Always taking his time. He would run Lizzy baths, with bubbles. He would do house chores, without even being asked. He had no money and no job, but Lizzy was lapping up all of the sweet tenderness that came with this man. She felt loved, wanted and safe. 9 months into the relationship Lizzy discovered that this lovely man, this Gentle Giant as he was known, was indeed a women beater and Lizzy felt the end of his fist. She was black and blue, her lip was split right through and she needed five stitches. The doctor found a small particle of his knuckle bone imbedded in her gum. You see Lizzy had a strong mind and was fiercely independent. She would stand up for what she believed in and knew that she could not continue in this relationship. She had been here before. Others and their emotions would not control her. She refused to back down out of principle. She had looked up to this man and had thought she had finally found what she had been looking for. She was devastated and emotionally torn, and kept it all to herself. She cried herself to sleep every night for weeks. No one knew what she was feeling or what she was going through. She kept a brave face on it. Not even her best mate, Sam, was aware. He begged and cried and promised that it would never happen again. But Lizzy was far too strong for this man. She locked away her love for him and told him where to get off! The emotional scars took far longer than the physical scars to heal. But Lizzy knew she would get through it. She became stronger.

With ice in her heart she refused to date men. She had

her male friends and that was enough. She knew that she had to wait until she was ready to give love again. She often thought that she had become frigid, but would dismiss that as a stupid idea. Instead she went to University. Whilst the other students were partying hard, Lizzy came home after a day of lectures. Lizzy would pick her daughter up from school, cook dinner and they would both study. Her daughter would read whilst Lizzy read. Everything was going really smoothly and Lizzy was happy. However, something was missing. Everything had become a routine and Lizzy was somewhat bored. She wanted more. She was never satisfied with what she had. In some cases that became her downfall. She was never scarce of male company, but wanted more than friendship. The men in her circle were not eligible candidates to receive Lizzy's love, or even her body. The ice had finally melted. She needed the warmth of a man's love, or maybe it was his groin. Yes, it was the groin; she just wanted passionate sex. It had been a while now and she was sick of sleeping alone. She wanted more. Then along came Ian.

Ian was a professional city worker. He was absolutely stunning, with a body rippling of muscles. Sex with Ian was dynamite. Lizzy could not get enough of him. However, Ian was up his own arse. He loved himself so much that he never had enough left for anyone else. But the sex was fantastic and at first that was all she wanted. Ian changed the goal post as he then decided that he wanted more than what Lizzy could offer and started pressurising her to get a job. He became quite horrible towards Lizzy and started telling her how she should dress. She was not a conformist and was proud of her individuality. It was important to her. If there was ever a walking advertisement for designer clothes, it was Ian. He was vein, conceited and selfish. Lizzy knew that a label did not make a person. She knew that the spirit, and we are not talking Jack Daniel's here, made the person. Lizzy started to realise just how shallow this man was. He also attacked her education that she was proud of. He said that she was not cut out for University and should leave. In other words he tried to say that Lizzy was stupid. Needless to say, Lizzy dumped him. No clothes were thrown out of the window this time, just a simple; you are the weakest link, goodbye, type of attitude.

Funny how things change as 4 years later, Ian was on Lizzy's doorstep. Now a father himself. Still up his own arse, but wanted a piece of Lizzy. This amused Lizzy and unconsciously she plotted a plan.

Lizzy was not one to let people, especially men, put her down. She knew that she had a lot to offer the right person, but was sometimes weak for sex. We've all been there! Come on even you! Good sex is hard to come by. If it's crap you adopt the philosophy that you are soul mates. People tend to stick together under this premise, scared to go it alone. Sooner or later one or the other plays away. Soul mates. Yes I know. Pathetic. Don't underestimate Lizzy. She knew that sex was not the be all and end all of a relationship. She realised that friendship and trust were imperative. She also knew that if it was not happening in the bedroom department, no relationship counsellor could make that one work! That's why when Lizzy had that chemistry with a man, she was in there before you could say foreplay. She definitely had that chemistry with Ian.

Lizzy decided to visit Ian with her degree in tow and feeling rather naughty. He had called her several times and invited her to his house. Ian's ex had walked out on him taking the baby. The house was empty. Lizzy put on her tightest pair of jeans that hugged every curve. She was a lot slimmer then, and had a very good physique. She still has, but has rounded out somewhat. She donned a beautiful black low cut top that showed off the curves of her 36DD breasts. Even though Lizzy had had a child, her breasts were still perky and full. They were one of her best assets and she was not shy to reveal them.

On entering Ian's house, Lizzy took off her coat and Ian could smell the sweet perfume she was wearing. She remembered that Ian loved this perfume. It drove him wild. It also made Lizzy feel exceptionally sexy. It's funny how certain smells can do this to a person.

When Lizzy felt sexy, she knew exactly how to home into her feminine side. She knew what to do and had great extreme pleasure in making a man squirm with ecstasy. It was not until she was in her late 20's that she realised how powerful a women can be. She was more confident now and sexually aware. It was a bit late coming for her, but she was so glad she had found it. Not only was she pretty, with an hour glass figure. She was intelligent and knew her own body. When she was in this mood, men could not resist her.

Ian poured the drinks and was playing soft music. The evening was very relaxed and sensual as Ian massaged Lizzy's shoulders. She was enjoying every moment. She had not been touched intimately for a while. She was very tempted to have sex today, as she recollected just how good they were together. But for some reason, Lizzy felt strong and was not going to give in. Well not totally anyway. The mood had been set with candles and Ian was hampering on with what ifs.

"What if", Lizzy said to him "I show you something?"

Ian was puzzled but well up for anything by this stage. Lizzy stood up and started to sway her hips to the slow soft music that was playing. Whilst she swayed her hips seductively, she then started to caress her body, slowly and gently. Ian stood up and wanted to join in and Lizzy told him to sit down and watch. As Lizzy went through the lap dancing motions it became quite obvious that Ian was getting very excited indeed. She leant over to Ian and gently kissed his lips and beckoned him to gently caress her firm buttocks, while she wriggled her womanly figure up and down like a snake. Ian face showed signs of ecstasy, as Lizzy rubbed his chest and shoulders, carefully stroking him and lingering with her touch.

By this time Ian was gagging for it. Lizzy stopped suddenly and declared that she had to leave as it was late. Ian begged her to stay. He held her close and kissed her tenderly on the neck and cheeks. Lizzy pulled away. She knew that she could not stay any longer. She did not want to. She had completed her mission. Ian knew that her daughter was at her mum's for the evening and she did not have to leave. She put her coat on and once again softly kissed Ian on the lips, and ears and neck. She then left the house, got into her car and drove home. On the way home she was thinking about how she had become a seductive vampire that evening and the thoughts of this made her feel good. *You go girl* Lizzy said out loud. She felt good inside knowing that she did not give in to temptation. She felt strong. She was glad that she did not give him the satisfaction of having her. No, she was better than he was and he was not worthy of her.

She had not been in 10 minutes when she heard knocking on the street door. Lizzy was shocked, as it must have been 1.30am. Ian was shouting very loudly through the letterbox.

"Lizzy let me in, please let me in"

Lizzy knew what he wanted. She had worked him up so much that the sex would have been explosive. But instead of letting him in she ignored him. Her unconscious plan had turned out better than she had expected. This was a great way for the man who loved himself, to be knocked off his pedestal.

Lizzy chuckled to herself and thought *you bitch*, as she heard his BMW drive away. She never heard from him again.

Lizzy was not a vindictive person, far from it. But men were her down full. If she felt that chemistry she would jump right in and not worry about the consequences. The smell of testosterone drove Lizzy wild. Some men have a distinct smell and, well, some men just stink. Have you ever had that chemical balance with a man where afterwards you smell of pure raw sex? Yep, that will be the testosterone. Lizzy loved that smell. There was also something about orgasms that Lizzy could not get enough of. Some men could give you triple orgasms whilst inside you. Then there are the other kind. The ones who don't have a clue and you end up finishing it off yourself. The few in between that sometimes get it right are the kind that get lucky. With each failed relationship the harder Lizzy became. She still was capable of love and caring, but she tried to keep a lid on that side. Emotions always got her into trouble and she always fell in love with the wrong man. Not that   she has had lots of men or lots of loves. But she was weak to men. She knew if she was strong, they could not touch her. She knew that she would woo and overpower them with her great art in the bedroom. Yes, Lizzy was a bit of a girl. Sex had to be fun, passionate and downright dirty. Men loved it.

Chapter 4

Every girl dreams of a white wedding and that Knight in shining armour. Yes even you. I don't think that we ever get over it. Lizzy dreams of getting married standing in the Indian Ocean, wearing a white bikini, designer of course, and a veil. She was such a romantic at heart, but lost belief. She did not really know what she wanted from a man, but knew exactly what she did not want. She took people for who they were and if she did not like them then she would not give them her time. This worked well for Lizzy. She got shot of many a looser before any damage was done. She was very fussy with the company she kept, especially with affairs of the heart. But when Lizzy was in love she was a different person.

As the time ticks in our lives, we tend to hanker less and less over the whole happy ever after scenario. The older we get the more grateful we become to a good night's shagging. And what a result, if a good shag comes back for more. You get a man like that and who needs gym membership.

Lizzy loved men. She loved sex. She loved to feel a man's skin on hers. She loved the caress and she loved passion. Passion was building up in Lizzy. It was always there inside her. It had taken a while for her to like sex. Her experience with her first love was not exactly tender. She had not realised at the time, as he was her first lover. Previous to that she was sexually molested at the age of 9 and raped by a neighbour at 11. In each case they were in their twenties and seemed to think that this was normal behaviour. Her early experiences had made it difficult for her to know what to expect. She had associated sex as being dirty and horrid. She had slept with her first love, the father of her child, because she thought that she should. She did not really want to, but after 6 months of dating she thought that was the next step. He did not make the process any easier and took her virginity without a blink of an eye. Consequently she had not really enjoyed sex until she began to have a few lovers and that was in her early 20's. She also had a few bad lovers. She had met one particular guy who was about as passionate as a gold fish. That was enough to kill any burning flame. Picture the scene. This man was very solvent, fit and good looking. He was a contractor where she was working and he would often talk to her, and asked her out on more than one occasion. He was very persistent and she gave in. He took her on numerous dates. The nice kind. She could get dressed up to the nines, in her slinky black little dress. He took her to fancy restaurants and then paid. She had the finest of wines and the very best food. They had not had sex yet and on this particular occasion they played footsie under the table, teasing each other on what was to be. Well this man was a scouser. There was something about his accent that Lizzy loved. It was a real turn on for her. Unfortunately he was a real turn off. His idea of a mad passionate night was wham bam thank you mam. And that was it. No wonder at the time her only best friend was her rampant rabbit. You have bad sex, or if sex is not existent, the good old friend is always available to play. Unless of course you forget to renew the batteries and then all hell lets loose! The worse part of the scouser experience was the fact that his two young girls walked into the bedroom just as he rolled off. Two young girls that she had never met before. Two young girls that gave her that strange innocent look of 'who are you, and what are you doing in my daddy's bed'. This man was so dumped.

I mentioned about men paying. Why is it that when guys take you out they expect you to pay for yourself? Come on guys. You really think that you can get into a women's' knickers by going Dutch. Men are a different breed. They know we like to be treated as an equal, but forget that we are ladies. There's a favourite saying of mine that I like to remind these tight fisted gits. Treat a woman like a lady and you will get the best out of her. To all the women out there. You know exactly what I am talking about. To all the men, take note. Where do men get off with that? Tony was an eligible bachelor. I remember this clearly as he was dating my mate Sam, prior to the idiot she is living with now. Well she had met him once and they were going out for a second date. Lizzy being the nosy one offered to drop Sam off to meet her date. Why did he not pick her up? He took her to a local Indian restaurant and ordered a bottle of Libframilch. Ouch! That went down like a led balloon. Do men not realise that once you hit 30, that women are actually more sophisticated than that. Professional, solvent women go out and drink Crystal champagne. Of course they do. Client functions, if nothing else, mature the pallet to the finer things in life. There is nothing worse than a man that buys cheap wine. It's a statement of either, you are not worth more, or he is stupid. After the meal, Tony asked for the bill. Sam said that she only had small change on her. She should never have mentioned that she would contribute. Why do women do that? We complain that men should pay, and then offer to pay. It does not make sense. A lesson for the girls. Do not offer to pay. If a man wants to take you out. He should pay. I know some women who say that if they pay then they do not owe them anything. You don't owe them anything anyway. They wanted the pleasure of your company, and that is what they got. Why an earth would Sam want to contribute to the cheap wine. I suppose she was being polite. Not for long. Tony decided that he would have a look in her purse and take the money out to pay towards the bill. Now if that were Lizzy, he would have been thumped. Sam, being the more lady out of the two, left the restaurant and dumped him by text.

Lizzy wanted it all. The house that she bought, the car that she bought, the daughter that she had, the job that she got, and the man of her dreams. She had everything else but was finding it difficult to find a man of her dreams. The type of man that opens a door for you. A man that takes you to a nice restaurant and not the likes of the Harvester. A man that treats you occasionally to a bouquet of flowers or a small gift of their appreciation of you. A man who makes you feel like a million dollars. A man who can't take his hands off of you and knows exactly how to drive you wild with passion. Where are these men? Men today want you to pay for yourself, want you to wear sexy underwear, but want you to buy it yourself, and then they expect a shag because they are there. They don't open doors for you, don't pick you up for your date. Instead they tell you to meet them half way down the central line and then send you home on the night bus, after you have spent the night going Dutch. Or, they come to your house empty handed, eat all of your food and drink all of your wine. And then, yes they want to watch the football, while you do the washing up. What joy these guys bring to our life. Not.

What ever happened to foreplay? It's not just about sex as foreplay. What ever happened to the art of conversational foreplay? It's called the chase or the game. Women love to be chased. *Don't we girls*? It gives us that sense of being wanted. Unfortunately sometimes it's not worth the hassle. The excitement, the anticipation and lusting can be dampened by the actual bedroom performance. Simon. Oh the lovely Simon. He chased Lizzy for months. He would call her, send her cards in the post, take her to nice restaurants, buy her gifts, pick her up from her house, and drop her home in a taxi. They would flirt and flirt some more. They would brush past each other, just so they could have some form of intimacy. It became electric. Until the moment of truth. Lizzy decided that she wanted Simon more than ever. She had fantasised about it. Her and Simon in the throes of passion. She was sure it would be that way. On leaving the restaurant, Lizzy invited Simon into her home. He had never been inside her home before. Her daughter was staying with friends and she was in the mood. Her powers of seduction were in full force. She threw a hook and reeled him in. It was intensifying, and then nothing. Simon could not get it up. It was flopping like a defrosted sausage. All limp and pitiful. Lizzy put it down to pressure and thought that she would give him another go at a later date. And she did. She gave him the benefit of the doubt. This time, he was a two-stroke jockey. All over in 2 seconds flat. What a disappointment for Lizzy. Needless to say she dumped him.

Lust, what a wonderful feeling that is. When the body aches for the other person, to such an extent that anything goes. People tend to confuse lust with love. Lizzy knew the difference all right. There was no comparison.

Yes, Lizzy wanted it all. She was determined to get it. Surely there are men out there that are this way in nature. Or are they the gay ones. Who knows? Lizzy was destined to find out.

Chapter 5

Lizzy had taken 2 days off from work. She wanted to get herself ready for the girlie holiday. She was half looking forward to it but was also a bit anxious. Lizzy was never one for the girls. She never really hung around with a great deal of them. She found them bitchy, competitive and full of shit. There were only a couple of females that she actually took to and has been friends with them for years. Ordinarily, she'd prefer a man's company. Not just for sex, but generally. She thought of herself as being one of the lads. Guys would befriend her and tell her all sorts of things. She learnt a lot about men from men. What they like, what type of women they like, and what lies they tell to get them out of a situation. Yet, she still loved men. Whilst her daughter was growing up she had around 10 men friends. They would pop over in the evenings and bring a bottle of wine. Not all at the same time, but sometimes two. They all knew about each other. Lizzy had nothing to hide as they were only friends and she was not having sex with any of them. In fact the closest they got to her was a kiss on the cheek goodbye. She would have intelligent conversation about life and its ups and downs. Occasionally, one of them would think that they were in with a chance. But Lizzy never had relationships with these guys. She knew instantly whether they would become a friend or a lover. She always found a lover outside of her male friend circle. I am sure that the neighbours thought she was some kind of hussy. But she did not care what people thought of her. She was her own person, in her own world, in her own life.

This holiday was going to be a totally new experience for Lizzy and she had a moment of excitement. She was going to go with it. She was hoping that everyone would get on and that they could have lots of fun.

Lizzy packed a gym bag and decided that she would have a swim, steam and Jacuzzi, before coming back to the house to start her packing. Already she was in a panic. What should she take, will it be warm. What will the girls be taking? Should she take condoms? *Who was she kidding with that question* she thought? *Of course she'll take condoms.*

As she got into her car to drive to the private gym, she was still pondering on what to take with her on her holiday. She was glad not to be at work. She was glad for a day of. Work had been so manic and she had secured a new contract for the biggest client the company had had. She thought of Luke and pictured his toned body, beautiful smile and sparkling baby blues. She felt a longing for him. She dismissed the thought as the traffic lights turned red. Slowing down to a halt, she put the radio on. There was a talk show on and they were speaking about significant others and the wonderful things they do and say. She changed the station and carried on with her drive. Her favourite song was playing and she turned up the volume and sang at the top of her voice until she reached the gym.

The swimming pool area was rather empty and she was happy that she could have a lane to herself. She wanted to swim. Lizzy loved swimming. It gave her clarity of mind. She had a routine. Even though Lizzy was not one for routine, she liked this one. Swim 30 lengths, 15 front crawl, and 15 breast stroke. 10-15 minutes in the steam room, olbas oil to hand, and then 10 minutes in the Jacuzzi. This was like heaven to Lizzy and she loved every minute of it. Sometimes if a lane was not free she would steam first, and wait patiently

Today felt different for Lizzy. She succeeded her lengths with ease and felt good. After her steam she sat in the Jacuzzi. Her mind drifting, her body relaxed. She looked around and saw three other people in the Jacuzzi of whom she did not know. Two guys and another female. All three were staring into space as if they were not on this planet. Lizzy started to chuckle to herself and thought that if these four people were in the Big Brother house, there would be no viewers. No one spoke to each other and it felt strange. Then the guy sitting to Lizzy's left broke the silence.

"What is in the small bottle you have?" he asked.

Lizzy told him about the benefits of olbas oil in the steam room. With that she chuckled again and told him about her Big Brother thoughts. The pair of them laughed and then they continued in conversation. They spoke about cultures, travelling and how reserved the English are. Lizzy looked at this guy and thought that he seemed nice. She should have left the Jacuzzi by now and already be on her way home. But something drew Lizzy to this man. He was kind, a bit quirky, but pleasant. He had a lovely voice and spoke with an educated tone. A formal introduction then took place and then the conversation continued.

"Hi" he said. "My name is Kai".

"Hi. I'm Lizzy".

They shook each other's hand. Lizzy looked at the large round clock positioned on the far wall of the swimming pool. She was shocked. She had been chatting to Kai for over 2 hours and was already behind schedule. Yet, she did not care. She liked talking with him. He seemed to like talking with her. Kai and Lizzy had been talking about their favourite films and he said that he would bring some in for her to lend, next time he was in. Then to her amazement they had made an unofficial date of seeing each other the next morning in the spin class.

Lizzy left the gym and finally got home. She made a coffee and decided to make a list for the holiday. All the time she was thinking of Kai, and the morning's activities. Kai was a TV presenter and a trained chef. He also had a daughter and he was the same age as Lizzy. She kept thinking of his smile and how his face lit up with the laughter they had shared. Then out of the blue she began to panic. "Bikini's" she said at the top of her voice. Oh dear she thought and ran up the stairs to the bedroom. How many will I need? Panic over, Lizzy had found 5 bikinis in her bottom drawer and felt a bit better. After writing her list she realised that she would need to go shopping and buy some toiletries and yes the condoms. Lizzy pictured   Kai again. A very clear picture of him came to mind, practically naked apart from his swimming trunks. Lizzy had checked out his body discreetly, whilst in the Jacuzzi. He was quite fit, not a muscular type, but lean. She was not able to see what goods he had to offer as he was always covered by the Jacuzzi bubbles. I wonder if he is any good in bed, she thought to herself. She would not mind finding out. She would meet Kai in the morning. The class would start at 9.30 and then she could chat with him after. Lizzy was actually looking forward to seeing him. This is absurd she had thought. *Lizzy,* she told herself, *get a grip.*

Lizzy was not bothered about buying new clothes for her girlie week away. Instead she decided that she needed to buy a pair of sandals and sun tan cream. She had a problem with the sun, as she often suffered with prickly heat. Ordinarily Lizzy would visit the doctor and have an antihistamine injection to counteract the allergy. The doctor would always lecture her about the sun's harmful rays. She never listened. Lizzy loved the sun and the warmth on her skin. She loved to sun bath and adored her skin when it was golden and glowing. She also knew that the cellulite she had gathered on her thighs was nicely hidden by a tan, along with the stretch marks she had earned from becoming a mother. For this very reason, she used the sun bed once a week. Now she was looking forward to topping it up with the Mediterranean sun. The pure thought of basking with a good book gave Lizzy a warm tingle inside. Or was she still thinking about romping with Kai. He had not quite faded away from her thoughts just yet.

On her way back, Lizzy thought about her daughter. She always took her daughter on holiday, everywhere she went. She felt somewhat guilty now that she was jetting off to Spain without her. She could not exactly take her along. After all, certain activities were definitely not for children. Although she was 15 now this type of exposure was far too early. Next time, Lizzy thought, she will take her daughter somewhere nice, somewhere for kids. Florida perhaps. The guilt never lasted long as Lizzy justified the holiday in her own mind. She was also not sure of what she should expect from this holiday, so she decided not to expect anything, but go with   the flow.

Later that afternoon, whilst Lizzy was reading the Times, the phone rang. She did not want to be interrupted and often let the phone go to answer machine. Her justification was that people are sometimes too quick to get into your life, and quite frankly, at this moment in time, Lizzy could not be bothered with small talk. Unless it was the juicy kind. You know the type of stuff us girls talk about. New men in our life, new sex positions we have tried. Whether the hot date, turned out to be not such a sex god. The most talked about subject with new men in our lives is the size of their manhood and whether they know how to use it. The phone rang off and Lizzy got back to her article. This person was becoming persistent as her mobile was now ringing. Checking the caller ID, Lizzy saw that it was Jenny. She picked up the mobile.

"Lizzy get your glad rags on we are going out hun" said an exited Jenny.

Lizzy was not really up for a night on the town, but Jenny was insisting.

"I'll pick you up at 8.30. Be ready. I've found a quaint little bar in Leyton. It'll be fun".

Lizzy put the phone down and sighed. She could tell that Jenny was on a mad rampage and to be honest she really loved going out with Jenny. She was so much fun. Jenny was a beautiful women, size 12, good physique, blonde short hair and very very confident. Sometimes she bordered on arrogance, but knew what she wanted. *It would also be good for her to fill me in with her hot date she had had the weekend before. Something's telling me that it was not so hot.* Lizzy said out loud. Lizzy went to the bedroom to find something to wear. She chose cropped trousers, a sexy top and her 2 inch black sandals with a diamond cross bar. She was 5ft 8 inches tall and these sandals made her feel sexy and slender. Lizzy looked up to Jenny. She loved her confidence and just the general way she carried herself. She was also very impulsive, which ordinarily meant trouble. The only negative thing that Lizzy would say about Jenny is that she wore too much makeup. Although she wore it well, it was always caked on. Lizzy was more of a naturalist. She liked to wear a small amount of makeup, never foundation or lipstick, but bronzing powder and mascara. That was her lot. To be honest Lizzy was not really one for the art of makeup. She did not really know what she should wear to suit her face. Consequently she just applied what she knew how to, and it worked well.

8.30pm and Jenny appears in the cab. She had already drunk half a bottle of wine and Lizzy could tell by Jenny's excitable mood that they were definitely going to find some action tonight. All the guys loved Jenny. She attracted them without any effort what so ever. Lizzy admired that. Lizzy was more laid back. When the two of them got together, they would always create a whirlwind, guaranteed.

The bar in Leyton was not really heaving with hunky young bachelors. Lizzy and Jenny looked at each other, both thinking the same. Line up the Sambuca's! They were about to create the party. After 3 or 4 Sambuca's each, Lizzy started to relax. Jenny was telling her about the not so hot date. The red hot stud, she thought she had met, turned out to be nothing more than a wet weekend. The girls laughed hard at Jenny's disappointment. The laughter had started to attract people and Jenny and Lizzy got chatting to 2 guys. In Jenny's rude arrogant manner she told them all about their misgivings, but they seemed to love it.

"Let's move on Jen" Lizzy said.

Lizzy was getting a bit bored and wanted to party. The girls got a cab and went to the local club. Lizzy did not like this club much, but as she was half cut, she would happily bop away to the tunes the DJ was pumping out. The two girls walked passed the bar towards the dance floor. There were a set of stairs that led down to the dance floor and as Jenny attempted to walk down the stairs, she misses one and stumbles. Within a few seconds she had recovered her position and was looking rather embarrassed. Lizzy is in hysterics. Jenny embarrassment returned as a young man standing beside the steps said to her, "did you miss the step love" and laughed along with his mates.

Jenny being the quick whited one she was stated, "maybe, but I can't miss your face, you ugly fucker" with confidence in her stride she strolled off. Lizzy and Jenny were in bits of laughter.

After dancing the night away, Lizzy wanted to go home. Jenny was staying at Lizzy's house, but had met a fella. She had been talking with him on and off during the evening. *How come she always meets the fellas?* Thought a bemused Lizzy.

Lizzy and Jenny took a cab back to Lizzy's house and Jenny decided that she was going to go back to the cab to meet up with the guy she had met. Lizzy felt uncomfortable with Jenny's decision but decided to keep it to herself, after all she was a big girl and could look after herself.

The next morning at 8am, Jenny was banging on Lizzy's door. Smiling like a Cheshire cat.

"Oh my god" she declared. "I have had sex all around his shop. On the floor, on the desk, by the window, in the toilet. It was amazing. He was amazing".

Lizzy was laughing away as Jenny carried on with her story.

"Are you going to see him again Jenny?" asked Lizzy.

"Nah", she said. "He is married and I just wanted a good bonk, after that disappointment I had the other night. It is funny" she said. "All night I was telling him *that he wanted me,* I flirted with him constantly, whispered in his ear what I could do with him. Men, they are so easy. A bit of conversational foreplay and they are like putty in your hands".

Jenny loved a challenge and she loved a shag, more so she would always win over her conquest, if she wanted sex she would just go out and get it. No   questions asked. She reminded

32

me of a man. The same type of attitude. She really did not care.

"No match for me, Jenny the man-eater" she giggled. "At one point he asked me to go to the toilets with him in the club. The cheek of it. He must think that I am some kind of slapper!"

They both giggle as Jenny then remembered that she had to be in work for 9am. In a blind panic Lizzy grabbed her cars key and drove Jenny home. She only lived ten minutes away and Lizzy was in no rush to get to work, as she had booked the day off. Lizzy was due to fly to Spain the next day and had lots to do. They air kissed each other on the cheeks and vowed to catch up after the holiday.

Although Jenny was very confident and had the sexual appetite of a rabbit. Underneath she was very insecure. She seemed to think that playing a game, as she did most weekends, would get her a man. She knew full well that this was not the case, but pursued it anyway. She had a hard time when her daughter was born. The father of her child had tried to kill her and she had a few failed relationships after that. She was not unlike Lizzy. They had similar traits and a similar attitude, towards life and men. But still Lizzy really liked Jenny. She was honest and to the point. She was confident and generous. She would listen, and then butt in with her story of which would always be one better than yours. On the whole she was a good mate and a total scream to go out with. Lizzy hoped Jenny would find the love she needed. But in a pure selfish manner did not want her to settle down. Who would Lizzy go out to play with? None of her others friends liked Jenny, because of her arrogant attitude. They did not see that she was hiding behind a barrier, yet, none of Lizzy's other friends were as much fun, or the ones that were, were under the thumb and rarely ventured out.

Chapter 6

Lizzy got back to the house around 9 o'clock. She was looking forward to a nice hot shower. She felt hung over and tired from the evening's shenanigans. Kai, she thought. She was supposed to meet him at 9.30. By the time she had a shower and got her gym stuff together, she would have missed him. She felt apprehensive. She wanted to see Kai. Perhaps if she arrived at the gym for 10am, he would be in the Jacuzzi. She did not want to rush. Instead she made a cup of tea and ate a slice of toast with marmite.

She rang Shelley. "Oh bird, you all ready to rock and roll?" said Lizzy.

"Yes babe. I have everything ready. Can I still stay at yours tonight? It's easier all round" said Shelley.

"Of course. What time you coming over?" asked Lizzy.

"Around 7ish. Is that OK? I'll bring a bottle of wine".

"Ok, see you then" said Lizzy and put the phone down.

Lizzy would have liked Jenny to come on holiday. Jenny could not get someone to look after her daughter. Shelley was a good crack though. She loved to drink and she loved a party. She was a lot younger than Lizzy, 10 years in fact. That did not worry either of them. They had become close friends over the years. Lizzy also wished that Sam could have come. Sam was Lizzy's oldest friend. She was kind, considerate and very loyal. She was placid and sensible. She also had a daughter. Her significant other half, had a tight rein on her and she was often wrapped up in his life and his kids. She was a beautiful woman with a heart of gold. He was a complete wanker and took advantage of her good nature. But you know how it goes, love is blind. Nature would take its course and he would be history. It was just a matter of time.

Lizzy washed up the cup, plate and knife and went upstairs to shower. It was already 10 am and she had decided that she had definitely missed her unofficial date at the gym with Kai. She got her gym bag together. She fancied a steam. *That'll get the alcohol out of my system,* she thought to herself.

She ironed her jeans and a T-shirt, brushed her hair and teeth and set out for the gym. Lizzy had long blonde hair. She loved her hair. It was dead straight and silky with no split ends. She often tied it up, as blow drying it was a nightmare. Lizzy had only just learnt the art of blow-drying. She was never very good at it. She liked her hair long, that way she could tie it back and forget about it. She had tried the GHD's but to no avail. How do women do this every day she had thought whilst trying to use the straighteners. She never got it right and eventually gave up with them. They sat in her bedroom never to be used again. It was a shame though, although naturally beautiful she could have made a lot more of herself. She just did not have time. Not on a daily basis anyway. She would make the effort when going out on the razz. But as she liked to swim 4 times a week, it seemed pointless to spend so much time with hair and makeup. She always presented herself well. Clean clothes that matched. Nice shoes, a suit for work and jeans for the weekend. The belt had to match the shoes and co-ordinate with the jacket and top. Lizzy loved to wear her jeans. She had a favourite pair that hugged her body. She often would wear these with a nice tailored shirt and a sexy pair of boots.

It was 10.45 when Lizzy reached the gym. She knew for sure that Kai would not be there and she was disappointed in herself. *It's not like you made a promise to him Lizzy* she told herself. The words washed around her mind. On entering the swimming pool area, she could see that there were no empty lanes, so she went straight into the steam room. There were two other people in the steam room and they were staring into space. They both looked like they had the worries of the world on their shoulders. Lizzy threw some drops of olbas oil onto the steamer and the eucalyptus started to fill the air. With deep breaths she inhaled the oil. This totally cleared her head. After around 15 minutes, Lizzy became agitated from the heat. She left the steam and showered. The showers were by the side of the pool next to the Jacuzzi. Lizzy emerged herself into the Jacuzzi, closed her eyes and drifted away. She had positioned herself away from everyone and was facing the pool. The jets of water were massaging her stomach and she could feel the water disperse around to her waist. She tried to empty her mind, but the thoughts were disturbed by the vision of Kai. She turned around to face the others in the pool, and there sat Kai. She felt excited and nervous.

"Hi Kai" *she* said quite sheepishly then stood up and left the Jacuzzi. There was now a free lane and she wanted to swim.

She had swum two lengths front crawl and on her second length she could see Kai standing at the pools edge. She stopped and looked up at him. He bent down and said *Hi.* Lizzy almost gushed. She was sure that he would not be here. She was happy that he was. Kai climbed into the pool and started chatting away to Lizzy.

"Kai" said Lizzy. "I'm not being funny but I need to swim. Do you want to swim with me?" she asked. Kai was quite happy to swim a couple of lengths. They both stopped at the pool edge and carried on with their conversation. Kai was telling Lizzy about his family and his failed relationship. He was saying how great it is to be single. Whilst Kai was chatting away, Lizzy decided to exercise her legs. She knew that they would be talking for a while.

"I have bought the films for you Liz. Only thing is they are VHS and not DV*D's.*"

"Thanks Kai" said Lizzy "but I don't have a VHS player anymore". Lizzy was quite shocked that he had bought the videos for her to borrow and was also shocked at the ease of the conversation between them.

"I need to exercise Kai, do you mind walking up and down

the lanes. That way I get part of a workout and we can still chat?" asked Lizzy.

Kai was quite up for the idea. He also loved to talk. It came to light that they both had quite a lot in common. They both loved films and the cinema. They had both tried the religious route with the Jehovah witnesses. And better still they were both single.

Lizzy was trying to understand why they had spent the past hour walking up and down the pool, without realising the time, chatting away like they were best mates. It seemed weird to her that this man whom she barely knew, touched her spirit. Was it her spirit or was she just feeling rather horny again? Lizzy also knew that she was one for attracting the 'nutters' of society. *Tread carefully girl.* She could hear the words clearly in her head. Yet, she did not want to leave She knew she had to go back home and pack her bags for the holiday. Those dreaded bags. She also knew that she would probably pack them at 5am the following morning. It seemed that Kai did not want to leave either. So they did not. Instead they both jumped into the Jacuzzi and let the warm bubbles float around their bodies. Lizzy was contemplating asking Kai to come for a coffee so they could carry on with their conversations. She dismissed the thought as ludicrous. Lizzy wanted to get close to Kai. There was a definite attraction, for her anyway. It seemed that Kai could have been sitting on the fence. He did inform Lizzy that he was going to a club on Friday. He even told her where about he would be standing in the club. Lizzy was not sure whether this was an invite to come along. She guessed it was, but left it there.

"Kai I really have to go. It's now 1.30 and I have lots to do" stated Lizzy in matter of fact tone.

"OK Liz, listen I'll be here on Monday, around 1ish. I'll bring the VHS for you".

"OK" said Lizzy as Kai left the Jacuzzi.

Lizzy had arranged to meet Kai before even

thinking. She was not going to be there Monday. She would be in Spain. Before she could tell him. He was gone. Lizzy walked to the changing rooms feeling quite depressed. What if I don't see him again? If he only goes to the gym in the daytime, how will I get to see him again? Lizzy was in a frenzy. She wanted to see him. She wanted to see him more than anything. She could not believe she was thinking in this manner. She told herself, that she did not even know him. He's probably a player and she did not want a relationship. With that settled in her mind, she hit the showers.

She also remembered that she had met someone else in the gym. He was an old friend of her Uncles. They had got chatting as she had remembered his face. He was around 10 years older than Lizzy. It had white hair and small eyes. He seemed really pleasant. So when he asked Lizzy to go out she accepted. She did not think anything of it really. They were just going out for a meal. It was not a date.

Sometimes Lizzy can be so naïve. His name was Phil and he picked Lizzy up at 9pm. She wore a black mini skirt about 2 inches above the knees, black knee length boots and patterned fitted top. She had blown dried her hair and applied a small amount of makeup and was ready to go. Phil arrived in a lime green jumper that looked like it had seen better days and a pair of black trousers. At that point Lizzy should have guessed that this was going to be a weird night.

He took her to a fancy restaurant. It was quaint and had a fantastic view. Lizzy was not over impressed as the tables were too close together and Lizzy could hear the conversation of the table next to them.

Phil was the perfect gentleman. He ordered a bottle of Chablis. After they had ordered the courses, Phil started to talk about himself. In fact he spoke about himself rather a lot. Lizzy was getting a bit bored and tried to get into his conversation. Lizzy then realised that Phil thought that this was a date and she was rather put out and started to feel uncomfortable. Phil kept jabbering on and then he talked about his prison sentence. *Oh god thought Lizzy, another nutter.* As these words circled her brain she looked Phil in the eyes and she could surely see that this man was a complete psycho. At first she felt a little frightened of him, but then came over with a calmness. He was only a bloke and he was trying to impress her. He had a funny way of doing that she had thought. She was not impressed, but rather mortified. She hid it well, and got him to change the subject. To make matters worse, he started talking about his ex, who Lizzy just so happened to know. *Great* she thought *things could not get any worse.* Lizzy ate her starter and wished that the main course would be there soon. She was getting annoyed that the waiter kept taking the bottle of wine away and that she had to wait until her glass was empty before a refill. Not just empty, but sitting on the table empty for a good 10 minutes. Lizzy told Phil of the annoyance this was causing her and it changed the subject to lighter matters, such as the food and the wine.

She could not wait to get out of there and go home. Phil dropped Lizzy home. She was surprised that he decided to drive after drinking two bottles of wine. She just hoped she would get home in one piece. She did. Phil stopped the car outside Lizzy's house. Then low and behold, Phil moves in for a snog. Lizzy stomach turned at the mere thought of it, and she had not realised, until that point, how much she did not like him. Even thinking about this now makes her want to throw up.

Lizzy sees Phil occasionally at the gym. He has no idea what she thought about that night. She palmed him off with the 'I'm still in love with my ex 'routine. And thankfully, that got shot of him.

Chapter 7

After her pool walk Lizzy felt rather peckish. It was late afternoon, and she had still not packed. Shelley was due around 7ish. She decided to make some Pasta. She was not really fond of pasta. Yet it was quick and easy. She put the water on to boil and made a cup of tea. She really fancied a glass of wine but abstained. She sat down in the kitchen, staring out of the window. She had a lovely view from her kitchen window. She could see the reservoir just beyond the electricity pylon. The pylon obscured the view, but it was not totally spoilt. The weather was pretty grim. Cloudy and cold. She thought about the holiday and the warmth of the sun on her skin and this bought a smile to her face. Just as she started to smile she then thought of Kai and wondered again whether she would see him again. In the same stretch of thought she started to ponder as to whether there would be any single eligible bachelors in Spain. She was not one for holiday romances, shag maybe, but even then she was rather fussy. That was half of her problem. Although she loved sex, she would not put it about. She was quite reserved and particular about whom she slept with. Some of her mates were not so particular. If it had a pulse and could get an erection, they were there. The water had started to boil and she added some salt and a drop of Olive oil. She added the pasta and waited for it to simmer. The tea was horrible, and she decided to open the wine anyway. She poured herself a glass of Rioja and put the lid on the saucepan. For speed Lizzy always had a packet of dolmio in the fridge. You know the kind that you can pop into the microwave for 60 seconds. She chose bolognaise with no extras. She was not fond of this sauce either. After a sip of wine, the pasta was ready and she sat down to eat.

She was not enjoying the food and would have rather eaten a roast dinner. Lizzy could not be bothered to cook a roast dinner. But now she wished she had. Lizzy was a fantastic cook. She loved to cook spicy dishes, but would rarely cook just for herself. Her daughter often ate out, or at a friend's house. She also liked to cook for her   friends. They appreciated her efforts. She did not have any speciality dish, but liked to experiment. She did have a love for Chicken and would marinate it the night before cooking.

Just as she was finishing her food the phone rang. It was Gina.

"Hola Lizzy, have you got everything ready?"

"No, I still have to pack. Shelley's coming over to stay the night. What time is the flight?" asked Lizzy

"12 noon" said Gina. "I am so excited. Gemma and Trish are here".

Lizzy could hear them shouting hello in the background.

"So Gina if the flight is at noon, we have to be there for 10. We should not have to leave until 8. It should not take 2 hours to get there?" questioned Lizzy.

"Ok" said Gina. "We'll get to yours for 8 then. Hasta Leugo". She giggles as she puts the phone down.

Lizzy decided to have a bath and wash her hair. Even though she had steamed and showered at the gym., she wanted to chill out with a glass of wine. She had also assumed that Shelley would want to use the bathroom. From previous experience, she knew that Shelley took no prisoners when using the bathroom. Bathing also relaxed Lizzy. She would often drift into her own world, where it was safe and calm.

She poured Imperial Leather, double bubble into the running water and placed the glass of wine on the side. She placed candles by the edge of the bath and recalled the time when she and Chris bathed together. They did not bath together often, but on this particular occasion he had rolled a spliff. Lizzy made sure that she sat at the end without the taps. She always made sure of this. On thinking about it she saw it as being a bit evil. But her logic was, it was her bath. So it   became her right to have the comfortable end. It was actually quite awkward but somehow they managed to both fit in the bath and relax. Chris would fold a towel and put it over the taps. He had picked this tip up from being burnt by the taps on previous occasions. The thought of this made Lizzy smile. For some obscure reason he would burn himself every time, before remembering to fold the towel and cover the taps. Lizzy wondered how someone could be so forgetful, especially when it caused pain. They sat in the bath for what would seem like hours, smoking the spliff, drinking wine and talking shit. Chris often spoke shit, yet he was an intelligent man. The weed kept getting wet and Lizzy soon gave up on even trying to smoke it. She was not a lover of it anyway as it made her think really deeply. Either that her made her a bit paranoid. She recalled the time when she was at home smoking with a friend. They were due to go out that evening. She was stoned and in total paranoia, to the extent that she could not leave the house although, she can laugh about these things now, it was quite scary at the time. Lizzy did not like that feeling, as she was quite a secure person in her own right. Well that's what she liked to think anyway.

Thinking about it Lizzy wondered whether smoking weed made you psychotic. When she had first met Chris, he was confident and strong. By mid relationship he was a complete wreck. She often wondered why, or how he had become that way. Was there a link with the weed? *Perhaps* she thought. That's why Chris stalked her.

She had finished the relationship but he refused to leave the house. So, she told him that she did not want to marry him.

She remembers Chris getting upset about what she said, and to make matters worse told him that she did not love him and would stay with him if that made him happy, but, she would not sleep with him and have torrid affairs elsewhere. Perhaps it was a combination of the weed and the insult. It was not because Lizzy did not love Chris. She could not deal with his insecurities. He was a very needy person, and she was not used to that. He always demanded her attention and time. He would go everywhere with her and did not like it if she wanted to go somewhere on her own.

On one particular occasion, Lizzy had had a really hard day at work. When she came home, Chris had cooked dinner. All she wanted to do was have a bath, glass of wine and chill out in her own world of calmness. She had run a bath, poured the wine and locked the bathroom door. The tension was just starting to release when Chris started banging on the bathroom door, demanding she let him in. She told him that she would be out in a while and he had tried to take the door of its hinges. That was the type of attitude she could not deal with. This was just one of the episodes as to why she dumped him.

Chris would smoke weed practically every day after work. His habit did annoy Lizzy, as it was a new habit that he had acquired. Perhaps he had a midlife crisis. After all he was 45, yet carried himself like an 18-year-old. Men never see that side of themselves, this is old git syndrome.

Men will never admit that they are scared of getting old. That's why they have affairs. It boosts their ego, and makes them believe that they are still a catch. Have you noticed that as guys reach puberty or shall we say 18+? All they want to do is chase girls. Girls are a conquest for them. They tell their mates all the details, and if there were no details they make them up. Some things never change. They reach mid 20's and then realise that they don't have to chase women, quite so hard. They start to realise the benefits between a quickie and a relationship. They are not so quick to hook up with anything and become choosier. They start to become confident with themselves. They are still young but mature enough to think about life. They reach their early thirties and are at their best. They are more prone to settling down and more experienced in life. They will still chance their luck, but are not too bothered. As soon as they hit the big 40, they become 18 again. Chasing anything that moves. This, gentlemen is called the male menopause. Yes, you guys get it too. They won't admit it, but they do change. If you ever get with a man that is in his 40's, beware.

Women are just as bad, she had thought. She knew women that pranced around in skirts up their arse, tits hanging out, long knee length boots, trying to pull anything and everything. These women made Lizzy laugh. They had no shame. Although they may have had nice figures, nothing could change their age apart from cosmetic surgery. Anti-wrinkle cream is not enough to make you look 20 again. They think they look good, it's is funny to watch them in the clubs. They wait about trying to chat up the guys. Young guys at that. The only action they get is when the guy has his beer goggles on and all he can see is her tits. She thinks she is in for a night of passion and he can't get it up because of the booze. But this does not stop these women. The following weekend they are out there again, trying their luck. It's sad really. Have they no class? Obviously not. She hoped that she did not get like that. God forbid.

Yet women had the same insecurities as men. They just seem to handle it differently. Once a women hits, 30, she is either devastated or in heaven. When Lizzy was 30 she loved it. She had really found herself and cemented the fact of who she was. She was not scared of getting old and was actually looking forward to hitting 35. She knew that at this time she would know she was a woman. Perhaps once she started to head towards the big 40, maybe she would think differently.

Women's insecurities surface in so many different ways. Firstly you get the women described above, flashing her bits and trying to pull anything. They are scared of being alone and think that because they get a shag, they are OK.

Some women hide behind their children. They do everything for the kids. Their life is the kids. They forget about themselves and before they know it, the children have all grown up and left, and they have no life.

Then there are the women who stay in a bad relationship, because they do not want to be alone. Time ticks on, and before they know it they are left on their own, with no life. Their former life revolved around their partner.

Lizzy was not so different to any of these women. She had her own insecurities, but   kept them well hidden. But at this stage in her life, she was not afraid of being alone. She had lived on her own for the majority of her adult life. It seemed that anytime she had lived with a man, it was not for long. She often wondered whether she could ever live with a man. Perhaps she was destined to be alone. He daughter was not far from grown up, but Lizzy still had a life. She had not hidden behind her child, as she had to earn the money to support her. She was certainly not one to mother a man either.

Lizzy had loved and been loved and she was happy with that. She also knew that she wanted to love again. She had often daydreamed about Mr Right. She thought Chris was her Mr Right. She was swept away with the romance of it all and not the reality. This was definitely the case with 'The Gentle Giant'. She would love again and feel love, she was certain of it.

Whilst the bath was running she went back downstairs and washed up the dishes from lunch. She knew she should pack soon and decided to do it after she had her bath.

Time was ticking and Lizzy placed her suitcase on her bed. Luckily for her she had a draw full of holiday clothes. These were clothes that she had bought just for her holidays. Every summer she hit the sales for the bargains. She put the iron on and started to prepare her case. She knew she could not take her rampant rabbit with her, as she would be sharing a room with Shelley. She was half hoping that she would not need it anyway. Whilst the iron was warming, she collected her toiletries together and put them into the suitcase, along with her makeup and condoms. Lizzy always put one Bikini, a couple of pairs of knickers and deodorant into her hand luggage, just in case her suitcase went walkies. This always worried Lizzy.

Underwear was packed along with her Bikini. She ironed her holiday outfits, a pair of jeans for travelling in, a black pair of trousers, two jumpers and her Jean jacket. Well, you can never be too sure, she thought.

It was already 7 0'clock and Shelley was late. Shelley was always late. Lizzy liked Shelley. They had clicked from the first day that had met. They were both working as Christmas temps and had hit it off instantly. Shelley was really funny, and a good laugh to go out with. She had a 'don't care attitude' and would strut around the bar like she owned it. They had nothing in common apart from the love of booze, men and the occasional club night. Yet, they remained mates. As she was younger than Lizzy, she was rather trendy. She would often go out in her jeans, designer only, and a designer top. She loved to flirt with the guys and was really good at it. She was pretty, about a size 14, with natural white blonde long hair. At 5ft 6, she was witty and intelligent, but would not be taken for a ride. Not by anyone. She would not think twice about thumping someone, be it male or female, especially if she had had a few drinks. She demanded respect and would give it back in return. If she did not get respect then you were not worthy of her time and she would make sure that you knew. Lizzy saw all of these attributes in Shelley, yet Shelley had never once disrespected Lizzy, or even acted this way towards her. They just had a mutual understanding and respect for each other. She was glad that she was coming on holiday.

Lizzy had drunk half of the bottle of wine and was wrapped up in her white towelling dressing gown. Choice fm was playing in the background and Lizzy done one last check of her case. Everything seemed in order and she chilled out on the sofa. Just as she sat down the doorbell rang and rang and rang. *Ah, thought Lizzy, that'll be Shelley.*

Shelley fell through the door, shoved her suitcase to the side in the hallway and gave Lizzy a big hug.

"Liz me ol ripper" she said slurring her words.

"You pissed already?" said a shocked Lizzy

"Yep, I'm on holiday and this is how I mean to go on" slurred Shelley

They both laughed. Shelley took the bottle opener and opened another bottle of wine. They sat in the living room and began their catch up. They had   not seen each other for a while and there was a lot to tell. Lizzy told Shelley about Kai and what had happened with Phil. Shelley told Lizzy about Seb, her new squeeze.

"Don't worry though girl" Shelley said. "Seb is not my bloke, he is my booty call. Whilst in Spain, I'm single. In fact unless he is actually in front of me, I'm single". They laughed together and reminisced.

The alarm woke Lizzy at 6.30am. She should have been used to getting up early, but she felt very tired this morning. She was also excited, as today was the day she was flying to Spain. She went downstairs and put the kettle on. Shelley was asleep in the living room on the blow up bed. Lizzy's daughter was also sleeping. She made the pair of them tea and toast and woke one at a time. Lizzy's daughter loved to sleep. She was definitely a bed merchant.

"Hey beautiful" Lizzy said to her softly stroking her hair. "Wake up, I have made some tea and toast for you. Come on, you have to get ready and go to nanny's". Forgetting she was 15 years old, Lizzy remained to stroke her hair and watch her beautiful daughter come to life from her deep sleep.

"Mum, get off, what you doing, get out of my room. Why you waking me at the crack of dawn. Just because you're going on holiday don't mean I have to get up, in it". Lizzy hated it when she spoke like that. Who ever made up that street talk should be shot.

"Come on babe, wake up. Here's your toast; it has strawberry jam on it, just as you like it" said Lizzy calmly.

Her daughter sat up took a bite and then complains.

"Eh butters, it's cold. I don't want it" her daughter shouted and threw it back on the plate.

Whatever, Lizzy had thought. She was relishing the day when her daughter came out of this stage. Teenagers are well,

47

bloody hard work. They talk a different language and expect you to understand.

Lizzy once threw her daughter back into the street and told her that she could not come back into the house until she learnt to speak properly. She remembers it well. Her daughter had come home from her friend's house, walked in the door and started speaking this street language.

"Mum, I went to blah blah init, and saw Derek, he is so Buff, his mate was proper butters, and he was cark. And that girl blah blah, is a bredder".

Lizzy did not have a clue what she was talking about, and the pure vocals coming out of her child's mouth, distressed her. She really did not think that this type of talk was appropriate and she hated it. She had learnt a bit herself though, she had to. She liked to know what the kids were talking about.

"Yeah and she's a sket" her daughter had continued.

Lizzy held her daughters arm, turned her around and marched her back out the front door. "Until you can speak English, you are not welcome in my house. So out you go. You can come back in when you have changed your vocabulary" fumed Lizzy.

For those who don't know, init, means hasn't it, Derek, was handsome, his mate was ugly and stoned, and the girl was a copycat, and also by all account a bit of a slapper.

Her daughter soon learned that this type of talk was not allowed in the house, however, they did sometimes joke about it between themselves. If there was ever a character that fitted the teenage persona, it was definitely Vicky Pollard from Little Britain. Lizzy loved that character, *yeah but no but yeah*. It made her chuckle every time she saw her. Although the character was a bit farfetched, it did sum up teenage hood so well.

Shelley was stirring in the living room.

"Hey hun, tea and toast. How are you feeling? We really knocked the alcohol back last night. My head is thumping" Lizzy had said. Shelley groaned and sat up. Lizzy knew she must have been feeling the same.

"I have to drop my daughter to my Mum's this morning. I'm gonna jump in the shower. While I'm gone you can have some privacy to get ready. The others are due here for 8 this morning. I'll pick the petrol up on the way" explained Lizzy.

Fortunately Lizzy had a 7 seater. It seemed strange that a two-person family would need such a big car, but it surely came in handy. Shelley grunted again.

Lizzy run the shower, her daughter had eaten the toast and got out of bed.

"Do you want the shower first?" Lizzy had shouted down the hall to her daughter. She knew how long it took her daughter to get ready. She certainly never got that from her Mum. The clothes had to be carefully ironed and the hair tied back so tight, she often wondered how it did not give her a headache. She had a 'slick' brush that would make her hair stick to her head and she would often take a small bit of her hair, drop it to the side and leave it hanging there. All the girls wore their hair this way. It was a trend. She also applied her makeup and it had to be perfect. Mascara eye shadow and lipstick. Something else that she had not learnt from Lizzy. Whilst her daughter was growing up, Lizzy never wore one scrap of makeup. She did not like it. But as she had gotten older, she tried to make a bit of an effort.

Lizzy showered and threw on the jeans that she had ironed the day previous. That was good for Lizzy, she normally ironed her clothes once she had decided what she was going to wear. Her daughter was very independent and ironed and washed her own clothes. Lizzy had made a point of teaching her this when she was younger. She wanted to make her daughter as independent as possible without turning her into a

49

loner. Lizzy knew the importance of this. She was not one to wait for people, she often went out alone, pictures, salsa dancing, shopping. She even went to the gym on her own. Her experience of people was that eventually they would let her down. She did not want her daughter to be let down. She loved her with all her heart. She was her life. Lizzy often had thought that she would not be where she was today if she had not had her daughter. It had made her strong, and it had made her experience the only true love that anyone can experience. Unconditional love.

Lizzy and her daughter jumped into the car and sped off to Leytonstone. Her Mum would be waiting, with a cup of tea ready. Lizzy was running late as her daughter's hair had not gone according to plan and she cursed as she took it all out again and restyled it. The journey only took 20 minutes because of the early hour. Lizzy still felt a tad tired and yawned loudly. Her daughter laughed and then there was silence. Lizzy gave her daughter 50 quid, and they hugged for what seemed like an eternity.

"Have a nice time Mum". Lizzy hugged and kissed her Mum and waved them goodbye.

On her way back she had those guilty pangs about leaving her daughter. She knew she would be safe and was grateful that her Mum was able to have her.

Shelley was dressed and ready to go. She was all excited about the holiday. They put the radio on and were dancing around the kitchen, wiggling their bums and hips and singing at the top of their voices. There was a voice shouting through the letterbox and it was Gina. Lizzy rushed to the door to let her in and she hugged her. Gina's friends were also with her. Trisha and Gemma.

"Lucy could not come" explained Gina. "Her ex is back in town and she is going to spend time with him".

Lizzy had thought this to be strange but dismissed even commenting. Why do women put things off, because of men? Surely he would be there when she got back?

50

Lizzy had not met Gina's friends before and discreetly gave them the once over. Although Lizzy was not judgmental, she could tell a lot about a person from their first meeting. Gemma was in her 30's. She was a mixed race girl, very pretty and about 5ft 6. She was quite petite and could only have been a size 10. She appeared very confident and very loud. In fact a bit of a party animal. She did not have any make up on and had dark circles under her eyes. Her skin had tones of yellow, as if she was slightly jaundice.

"I have not slept yet, Lizzy. Went out last night on the lash. There's a new club in town and I, as always, have to be one of the first to try it out". Gemma laughed as she finished her statement.

Trish was around 40. She had bleach blonde hair, about a size 14 and a big smile. She had a soft golden glow to her complexion and was a pretty girl. Lizzy thought that she was the quite one out of the three, as Gina was a bit of a party girl to at heart.

After a formal introduction, the girls started to chat about their lives, in general and how much they were looking forward to the holiday. Gina looked stunning today. Mind you she always did. For someone so naturally beautiful it was a shame that she had no confidence in herself at all. Lizzy did not understand why Gina felt this way about herself. But to be honest, had never really had a deep conversation with her. She knew that Gina was at her happiest when she was the centre of attention. She liked to be admired and praised.

Lizzy used to let her get on with it, and stay in the background. She was not one for centre stage. Well not until she was pissed and then all hell would let loose.

After, one last check, of tickets, passports and money, the girls loaded the 7 seater and started their journey to Gatwick airport. The flight was a 12 noon and they had set off in good time. The radio was blaring and the girls were singing. Lizzy hated flying. Although she had travelled a bit she still hated flying. She recalled how it made her feel. Sick and light headed. She had a cure though. A good drink before she boarded. It calmed her nerves and relaxed her.

She parked the car at the airport and they unloaded. Lizzy was starting to feel excited now but she normally contained it until she got to the destination. She was thinking of the sun. The weather in the South West of England was awful. It was cloudy and dull and looked like the heavens were going to open up at any stage. They checked in and offloaded their suitcase.

"Right then" exclaimed Lizzy. "Let's hit the bar". Shelley was up for it, but the other looked absolutely stunned. Without further a due, Lizzy and Shelley found a nice spot, and both ordered a vodka and diet lemonade. After a few of those, the two girls started to feel a little bit tipsy.

"We should go through to the departure lounge" said Gemma, and so they all wandered through.

Shelley went straight to the duty free shop and bought a litre of Vodka.

"Let's go to McDonalds and buy 2 lemonades, we can put the vodka in the cup. Sod paying £3.50 every time we want a drink" declared Shelley.

Lizzy liked her logic and the girls followed. They took their lemonade and sat outside the bar situated on the top level. There were a group of lads, playing music from a small CD player, and Lizzy and Shelley homed straight in. The girls started chatting with the guys, and they soon realised that they were gay. Shelley shared her Vodka with the guys. As they were cracking jokes and messing about, and then a last call came over the tannoy. The girls carried on with their conversations and then the announcement was repeated.

"This is the last call for flight number, BA 2751 going to Spain, boarding at gate number 25"

. In sheer horror they realised that it was their flight. "Bye guys!" Lizzy shouted and they picked up their hand luggage and ran towards the gate number. Just their luck it was the furthest gate away. Out of breath, they reached the boarding gate and the stewardess looked upon the girls with absolute disgust. They all giggled together and boarded the plane. The plane was full and the passengers had been waiting for the last passengers to board before they could leave. Needless to say there were some very dirty looks banded about. The girls did not care, they were pissed anyway and it was only 12 noon.

Lizzy sat in her seat. It was an aisle seat. She strapped herself in and began to get palpitations. Although she was pissed it did not stop her thinking about plane crashes. She started to get rather hot. To ease her discomfort she imagined herself on the beach and told herself that it would all be worth it. As the plane took off, the entire colour in Lizzy's face drained. She clung onto the armrest and anyone would have thought she was on a white-knuckle ride. She sat straight-backed and eyes closed; constantly gripping the arm rests. It was not until about 20 minutes into the flight that she felt that she could relax slightly. All the girls were taking the micky out of her. But she did not care. She was not scared to show that she had a phobia. She knew that the phobia would not stop her from travelling and felt proud of that fact.

Lizzy hated planes. The seats were never wide enough and there was never enough legroom. She felt squashed and claustrophobic. She would not leave her seat, and kept her seat belt on through the whole journey.

After landing, and collecting their suitcases the girls headed for the coach that would take them to their apartments. The sun was shining and it was warm. Lizzy was a bit disappointed in the weather. It was around 60 degrees and she was hoping for 70 plus.

The apartments were great. In the centre of town. They had adjoining apartments. Gemma, Gina and Trish were in one and Shelley and Lizzy in the other. After inspecting each other's apartments Shelley poured a drink.

"Here you go Liz; you look like you need it" she laughed

The apartments were far from 4 star, but practical and clean. They were very basic. The lounge area was small. The sofa turned into a bed and it had a fridge and a two ring electric hob. There was no kettle or toaster. There was also a bedroom with two single beds and a tiny balcony that overlooked a building site.

The girls congregated into one apartment to discuss what they would do that evening. The time had flown by and it was already 7pm. A unanimous vote was dinner then clubbing. As you can imagine it took them ages to get ready.

Shelley and Lizzy were pissed again and giggling away like a couple of teenagers. They were having a good time and they did not care. They had contended with Gina prancing around the room every two minutes in a different outfit.

"Does this look OK? Does my bum look big in this? What about this?" After about five changes of outfit Gina finally chose the one she wanted to wear. Trish looked stunning in a silver cat suit that hugged her every curve. Her makeup was perfect and you could no longer see the yellow tones and dark circles. Gemma wore a pair of black trousers, a black halter neck top and a pair of high heeled sandals. She tied her hair up. She did not look her age of 40+, but rather early 30's. She had an air of confidence and sophistication about her. She definitely knew she looked good.

Shelley wore a mini skirt, knee length boots and a D&G tee shirt. She had no knickers on and was proud to tell us all.

Lizzy wore her jeans; a low cut top and cotton fitted jacket. She was not one for dressing up to the nines, unless she had to. She felt comfortable. She added a touch of elegance to her outfit with a beautiful diamond cross around her neck. She had the earrings to match. She tied her hair up in a bun and was ready to go.

Walking along the main street, there were touts everywhere trying to get the girls to go into their club. It was 10.30pm and they had forgotten about food. They found a nice open-air bar, went in and ordered cocktails. There was music in the background. The girls chatted for a while and Gina became bored. She wanted to go clubbing. None of the girls had been to this part of Spain before and were not sure what club to go to. They did not know what options were available. They did find out that as the season had not started yet, there would not be many options. They discovered that the most popular club, Benjy's, would be open. So they downed their drinks and headed in the direction of the club.

The club itself was quite big. There was a huge dance floor and three bars. It was rather empty and the DJ was playing mainly trance type music. Lizzy did not like this music at all, but decided to go with the flow. As always the first point of call was the bar. Lizzy and Shelley ordered a Vodka, Gina and Gemma ordered Jack Daniel's and Trish had a glass of wine.

Lizzy noticed that there were quite a few soldiers in the club. One of them was talking to Gina. Apparently he was a sergeant and an American. Lizzy liked the American accent. She was listening to the conversation and was hoping that Gina fobbed him off. Selfish cow, she had thought to herself. But she wanted to talk with the Sergeant. The girls walked around and then found themselves on the dance floor, wiggling their hips to Tom Jones Sex bomb. Before you could sing the first line, the soldiers were also on the dance floor, strutting their stuff. The sergeant started dancing around Lizzy, and two corporals were dancing around Gemma and Shelley. Lizzy decided to get naughty and was teasing the sergeant with her sexy dance moves. He was lapping it up and before you know it the soldiers were buying the girls a drink.

Gina had indeed fobbed off the sergeant and Lizzy had not felt so bad about her selfish thoughts. They chatted for a while and Lizzy was enjoying his conversation. She had found in the past that generally soldiers were quite intellectual.

The club never filled up, and was now shutting down for the evening. It was around 4am. The sergeant looked at his watch and then looked at Lizzy.

"Do you fancy a night cap mam?" He asked

The corporal that Gemma was talking to had also asked the same question. These two guys were sharing a room at the same hotel. After consultation the girls agreed to go back to the hotel.

The hotel was lovely. It had marble floors and a reception area with leather sofas. It also had fine decorative flowers in beautiful vases .It must have cost a bomb. It was also a good 10 minutes' walk from the club.

Gemma wasted no time and was on the bed playing tonsil tennis with the corporal. His hands were all over her. The sergeant offered Lizzy a drink. He only had Jim Beam, no ice or mixer. She took the drink. It was the first time Lizzy had drunk Jim Beam and she liked it. The sergeant and Lizzy laid on the bed, and he put the telly on. Lizzy's favourite film was on. Austin Powers. "Yeah baby yeah" she said laughing uncontrollably. The sergeant found this really funny because of her English accent, and the pair of them were laughing hard. Gemma and the corporal were getting down to some jiggy business and Lizzy felt a bit embarrassed. The sergeant wanted a piece of Lizzy but she told him that she was in a relationship. Although this was a lie she did not fancy him at all. Her lie had worked and they spent the rest of the evening drinking Jim Bean and laughing about scenarios that had happened to them in the past. She did not think that Gemma and the corporal was ever going to come up for air. The next thing she knew, it was around 8am and she realised that she must have fallen asleep. She felt cold, and wet. She looked down at her jeans and they were soaking wet. The sergeant woke and then jumped up as if to salute. He was also wet. She assessed the wet patch and noticed that it was on the top of her left leg and continued all the way down to her knee. She had slept on her right leg. First of all she dreaded the worst and then she realised that the sergeant had pissed all over her whilst asleep. He was totally embarrassed to say the least and he and the corporal proceeded to change the bedding. It was soaked through as they had slept on top of the covers with all of their clothes on. With all of the commotion going on, Gemma woke up.

"What's going on Lizzy are you OK? ". She asked.

"Get your clothes on girl, we have to leave" demanded Lizzy.

Gemma got dressed in a hurry and the girls left the hotel. Lizzy was covered in piss and had to walk back to the apartment. This was good twenty minutes away and she stunk to high heaven. At first they were unsure where they were, and decided to stick with the main roads.

"Can you believe that Gemma; he pissed all over me? "Said a disgusted Lizzy.

It had now sunk in and Lizzy wanted to throw up. She was still drunk and in total shock.

"We'll I had a nice time" said Gemma.

"Yes I know" said Lizzy. "I heard you".

The girls laughed uncontrollably, as they walked back the apartment. All the time Lizzy tried not to walk too close to anyone. She was totally paranoid about the stench. She could not wait to get back to the apartment so she could clean up. She was totally embarrassed and knew she would have to explain herself to the others.

She was even more pissed off when she realised that she wanted to wear those jeans on the flight back home.

Chapter 8

Back at the apartment, Lizzy took a shower. The water was cold but she knew she had to wash the piss off her body. She felt dirty and also sadness that a grown man still wet the bed. She had only been in Spain for one night and already she wanted to go home. She was missing her daughter and thinking about Kai.

The girls got ready and went for breakfast. It was around 11 am and they found a bar that had full English on the menu. It was now pouring with rain. All the girls were hung over and the topic of the morning's conversation was the pissy sergeant. The bad weather had put a dampener on the girl's spirits.

The holiday resort catered for sun, and there was not much else one could do apart from sunbathe, or party. Sleeping the day away also seemed out of the question as Gina insisted that everyone had to be awake, at what seemed like the crack of dawn, every morning to have breakfast together.

Lizzy was not one for sleeping for the sake of it, or sleeping in late. She was a busy woman with a lot of energy and found that she could not sit still for a long length of time. Trish disappeared from the table went to the bar and came back.

"I have ordered a shot of brandy for everyone" declared Trish. Gina was mortified and said "It's only 11.30 am! ".

"Yes, I know" said Trish "and" she continued "it's cold and wet and we need a livener. What do you reckon Liz? You must have a chill from sleeping in that piss".

The girls roared with laughter. The bar tender bought over the shots and before they had drunk them Shelley had ordered another, and then another and then another. They ended up drinking 10 shots each. As you can imagine, by this time the girls were rather drunk. Gina declared that she was not drunk and that she could drink brandy straight, like it was water and it had no effect. Gemma thought that it would be funny to add a little drop of coca cola to the next shot and get Gina to drink it. "Apparently" Gemma explained. "There is a 20% 80% rule, whereby, if you added 20% coke to the shot, it races around your body and made you drunk. It dilutes the alcohol enough for it to digest and enter the bloodstream quicker".

They all had one each and Gina knocked hers back, and another one and another one. By this time her complexion had changed from a pink glow to that of a dead person in a morgue.

"I have got to go back, I don't feel well" slurred a very drunk Gina. Lizzy helped her up and they wandered back to the apartments. They had literally stepped through the door and Gina heaved. Trish grabbed a saucepan and thrust it under Gina's face. Gina spent the next three hours throwing up. The jokes now revolved around lightweight Gina, and the memory of Lizzy being pissed on, was forgotten.

The girls sat around the apartment, wishing the rain would stop and talking about anything. Lizzy was becoming a bit bored and wanted to do something else.

"Who's up for going to Barcelona?" asked Lizzy. No one replied and they carried on with their conversations. Lizzy had heard that Barcelona had a beautiful cathedral. She had also heard that the nightlife there was really good. It was a train ride away, and she was not too sure if she could be bothered either. She would mention it again later in the holiday. If the rain continued they would have to find something to do!

Later that evening, the girls made a cocktail of Vodka, white wine, orange and Jack Daniel's. They all sat in the one apartment, Lizzy's apartment, talking about the soldiers. The Sergeant and the corporal had said that they would meet Lizzy and Gemma at the same night-club. Lizzy did not like the night-club and wanted to go somewhere else. She had stated the fact, but the girls wanted to meet the soldiers. Lizzy was not fussed. Gina was still feeling rough and would not drink the cocktail.

She also said that she might not come out. Trish said she would stay with her. Shelley, Gemma and Lizzy got ready for the night out on the town. Whilst walking along the strip, they decided to get a burger, once again being hassled by the club touts. They walked along to Benjy's and the corporal was waiting for Gemma.

"Sorry Liz, the sergeant is not coming out tonight; he does not feel well" said a rather embarrassed corporal. Lizzy had a sigh of relief and was not surprised. He must have been totally embarrassed.

Inside the club, Lizzy ordered a glass of wine. She was fed up with Vodka. Shelley was talking to another corporal. The girls had not seen this one the night before and he was young and handsome. Lizzy propped the bar up. She wanted to leave. She wanted to find a better club. One with better music. She did not like trance. Shelley was busy with her corporal and Gemma was not interested in the corporal from the night before.

"Gemma, do you fancy finding somewhere else? I really don't like it in here" said Lizzy. Gemma agreed.

They both spoke to Shelley. "Do you want to come?" Shelley wanted to stay with the corporal. The girls weren't happy about leaving her and asked her to bring him along. They left the club and walked along the strip. They came across another club called Black and White. They walked inside and the music was thumping. The DJ was playing R n B and Lizzy was in her element. She shook her hips as she queued at the bar. As she looked around all she could see was black people with their jeans down their backsides and their Calvin Klein underwear showing, donning baseball caps, or bandannas. For a second Lizzy thought she must be in New York.

She chuckled to herself and beckoned the others to walk around the club Lizzy had already consumed a lot of alcohol and she was rather tipsy. The DJ started to mix and Lizzy recognised the song that was being mixed in. All the New Yorkers were standing around with attitude, looking at the Gemma and Lizzy as if to say, *hey white dudes what y'all doing here.* A song started to play and Lizzy could hear the lyrics and was singing in her head.

Say what say what say what, yeeah, ohh girl you know what's up.

Lizzy grabbed Gemma and led her to the dance floor. She loved this record, Donnel Jones, Say What. They both started dancing as if they were one of the girls on MTV base. It became apparent that Gemma also loved this track. They strutted their stuff all around the dance floor and the New Yorkers stood in amazement. Lizzy thought, well us white people can also shake our toosh, and to be honest she was not bothered whether they were looking at her or not. Lizzy was a good dancer. She danced in time and had a few good moves under her belt. The fact that she was so drunk and did not even know what she was doing did not bother her. She was finally enjoying herself. As the next track was mixed in, Lizzy and Gemma both laughed out loud. They left the dance floor and went to look for Shelley. Shelley was nowhere to be found. They searched the whole club, including the toilets, and could not find her. They decided to leave and see if she was back at the apartments.

Gemma and Lizzy had a great time in Black and White and vowed to go back another evening. At the apartments, Gina was still white as a sheet but had stopped throwing up. Trish was by her side, rubbing her back. Shelley was nowhere to be seen. All four girls tried not to think the worst. They knew she was with the corporal and knew where the soldiers were staying. Lizzy was tired. She showered and went to bed, humming away to herself the Donnel Jones track. She had been asleep for a while and she heard Shelley come into the bedroom. The bedroom consisted of two single beds. She was still half-asleep and decided not to stir. It was not long before she heard a male voice. Then after a few minutes of silence she heard a slobbering sound. Lizzy thought she might be dreaming as she could barely hear this noise. She passed it off as something going on outside in the street. This continued for what seemed like 10 minutes and then she heard Shelley groaning. Still unable to wake up, Lizzy was not sure of what she heard. Once again, she tried to dismiss what she was hearing and put it down to too much alcohol. Sometimes, when she drunk too heavily, she would often hear or see things whilst she was drowsy.

The slobbering continued and Lizzy heard Shelly groaning again. It then dawned on Lizzy exactly what was going on. *Oh my God. They can't be!* Lizzy did not know what to do. Shelley and the corporal were having sex. Right next to her. They thought she was asleep. Well she was until that point. Should she get up and walk out or should she try to get back to sleep. Should she let them know she could hear them? She was so drunk and so tired that she couldn't have got up even if she wanted to.

With that last thought, there was a load groan from Shelley and a grunt from the corporal. She assumed it was the corporal. Then there was a silence, followed by a few whispered words and the she heard footsteps. Lizzy realised that the session must be all over and that the corporal was leaving.

Lizzy was shocked and was not aware that women did not mind having sex in the same room as their friends. She had always seen this as a private act between two people. This was the second time in two nights that she had been subjected to people having sex. *Was this normal?* She thought. At this moment in time she was past caring, she wanted to resume her sleep.

What felt like only a few hours later, Gina was banging on the apartment door?

"Wake wakey, rise and shine". Gina's voice echoed through the room. Lizzy looked at her watch. It was 8am and she needed at least another four hours sleep. Gina had let herself in and was in the bedroom, shouting at the top of her voice. Or at least that what it had seemed like. Shelley woke up.

"What's all the noise about?" asked Shelley

"It's time for breakfast. Come on everybody up" Gina

shouted.

It was raining again, and Lizzy hid under her covers. Shelley was shouting at Gina.

"Just because you are up it does not mean that we all have to get up!" Shelley then hid under her covers.

Gina stormed out of the bedroom and woke Gemma and Trisha. Lizzy could here Gina complaining.

"We should all get up and do something together. I'm not sitting up on my own and I'm, not going to breakfast on my own. The others are being totally unfair" Gina moaned.

Lizzy decided to get up so as to keep the peace, and Shelley followed suit. She was not happy about doing so.

Lizzy did not know if or how to approach the subject of last night's events with Shelley. She was still unsure as to whether it was the norm on a girlie holiday. So she decided not to mention it at all, unless Shelley wanted to talk about it. It was never spoken about, and Shelley never mentioned it.

Trish was mooching about feeling guilty that she had given Gina the mixed shots. She had said sorry about five times the day before and had now decided to do anything that Gina wanted. Of course, Gina was taking full advantage of her behaviour.

It took a few hours for the girls to wake up properly and get dressed. Lizzy was glad that she had bought her denim jacket with her, as it was cold and wet. They found a place for breakfast and ate plenty. Lizzy was still tired and told the girls she was going back to the apartment for a snooze. Ideally she would have liked to have fallen asleep in the sun. Shelley said she would go back with her and they trundled off together. They knew that Gina would be waking them up in a few hours, once she was bored with sitting in the café.

63

As they walked back to the apartments, Lizzy's was fast coming to the conclusion that this holiday was a bad idea. She was still in shock about the events that had occurred and could not quite get her head around it.

This is supposed to be fun? These words rolled around her mind. She vowed never to go on a girlie holiday again.

She lay in her bed, with her blankets wrapped around her tightly. She was thinking of Kai, and wondering when she would see him again.

Chapter 9

Just as Lizzy had expected, Gina was pounding on the door two hours later. "Lizzy, Lizzy wake up" exclaimed Gina.

Lizzy stirred and turned around to face Gina.

" We are going to play cards" she said. "Do you fancy joining in?"

Lizzy could not believe that she had been woken to play cards. How dull, she thought.

"Let's go into Barcelona". Lizzy tried again. Gina was not happy to go to Barcelona. Gemma did not want to go. Neither did Shelley.

"I'll come with you. It's got to be better than sitting in the apartments" Trish said.

Thank the Lord. Lizzy thought. At least someone wants a bit of the culture.

A very groggy Lizzy got up from the bed and put on her combat trousers, trainers and a jumper. She grabbed her Jean jacket and they headed for the station. They agreed to meet the others at 'Cheers' bar near to the station at the resort.

The map on the station wall was easy enough to read and the train arrived quite promptly. It was mid-afternoon and although the rain had stopped, there was no sunshine to be seen.

"You know Trish; I have always associated Spain with sun. What a disappointment this has been" said a disappointed Lizzy.

"If you want the best weather, you need to be in the South. Apparently, they get more sun" said Trish.

Lizzy was totally unaware of this, and was not even sure if she was in the South, but she made a mental note in her head to remember that little fact, next time she decided to have a holiday in Spain.

The journey took around 20 minutes and before they knew it they were there.

Trish seemed a lot quieter than she had been previously. Her dark circles had returned, as she was not wearing any make up. Her voice was husky from the lack of sleep and alcohol abuse. It had surprised Lizzy that she was quite an intelligent girl and was full of mindless facts and figures. They came out of the station and followed the exit. All around them were shops and more shops. It reminded Lizzy of Oxford Street. There was lots of Mediterranean looking people walking around. They had a more relaxed approach to that of people in London and walked with ease instead of briskly. The sky was grey which made it seem darker than it really was. Lizzy and Trish both agreed to find the cathedral. They knew it would be in la plaza, and searched for signs on the road for directions. They wandered around for a while and then found their bearings. The cathedral was located in the Placa de la Seu in the Barri Gotic district.

The cathedral was huge with variable points leading as far up as the eye could see. It was a magnificent piece of architecture and very gothic in its appearance. Lizzy thought that this was a strange concept for a cathedral as she always associated anything gothic looking to that of the 'dark side'. Although not religious she was very spiritual and moral. She would pray regularly and felt that there was some divine being that protected her. The cathedral was dedicated to the first patron saint of Barcelona, Santa Eulalia. She was tortured to death by the Romans, in the 4th century, because of her religion. Trish and Lizzy looked at the cathedral in awe. The octagonal clock tower reached massive 50 metres and the spire of the central tower was over 230 feet high. There were a vast number of steps leading up to the entrance and they both wanted to go inside.

Inside the cathedral there was a choir singing and a quartet playing. The two girls sat on a chair beside each other and breathed in the atmosphere. It was certainly uplifting and had a deep sense of spirituality about it. Lizzy felt calm, relaxed and fulfilled. She felt at peace with herself and at one with herself. It was not often she had that feeling of wholeness. She was always lacking something in her life, or so she thought, and consequently trying to achieve more and gain more, and live more. Sometimes she wondered how she had the time to fit everything in the way she did.

Lizzy loved culture. She loved to exhume the cultures of different cities around the world. Most of her friends were not really into that sort of thing, so when she did get a chance to explore she would. Trish appeared bored and asked Lizzy if they could leave. The two girls left the cathedral. Lizzy wanted to explore it in more depth, and vowed to herself to come and have another look at another time.

On leaving the cathedral, the girls decided to find a café. They were not sure where to go and wondered around the plaza for a while. Lizzy took one last look at the cathedral in all its glory, before leaving the square. They walked slowly around the streets and found a small café in a back street. They could see that they had stumbled into the back streets of Barcelona, and Lizzy was quite pleased that she could sit with the locals. Trish gave the impression that she was not comfortable with being away from the tourist spots, but sat down anyway.

The waiter came to the table. He was olive skinned, with a round belly, and dark short hair. He also had a moustache, and was in his late 40's.

"Hola Senorita" he said with a smile.

"Hola Senor, dos café con leche, por favor" said Lizzy

"Si, Senorita, con azucar?" he questioned.

"Si, con azucar" Lizzy said smiling.

The waiter walked off and Trish was looking at Lizzy in amazement.

"I never knew you could speak Spanish. What did you ask for?" stated an amazed Trish.

Lizzy laughed. "I only speak a little Spanish and asked for two coffees with milk and sugar" she explained.

Trish smiled widely. *"What if I did not want coffee?"*

"I can ask for something else if you want" said Lizzy.

"Nah only kidding" said Trish playfully.

The waiter returned with the coffee and Lizzy asked how much, and paid the 3 euros.

Whilst the girls were sipping their coffee they realised that they were being watched by two guys behind them on another table. They were chatting in Spanish and Lizzy could barely make out what they were saying. *Damn* she had thought to herself. *Why do the Spanish speak so fast? I must get past this beginner's course.*

Trish started to become more uncomfortable with the situation so they decided to leave. Just opposite the café appeared to be a YMCA, or a hostel. There were a few Spanish men standing about outside the hostel entrance. Lizzy grabbed Trish by the arm and beckoned her to walk with more speed. As the girls found their way back to the square they both sighed in relief. They remembered the way back to the train station and were amazed to see that it was 8 o'clock in the evening. They had not realised that they had been gone for so long.

On the train, Trish and Lizzy chatted away as if they were old pals. Lizzy was not one to let people get close to her. She liked to keep her distance from both men and women.

68

However, when she liked someone she would open up completely. If they abused her trust in any form, she would no longer associate with them. Hence, Lizzy had a few select people in her life and that was the way she liked it. She did not suffer fools gladly.

The journey did not take long and they trundled off to the bar that they had agreed to meet in.

Gina, Gemma and Shelley were inside the bar. Lizzy looked around. The bar was huge with plants everywhere and tables and chairs neatly stacked around the floor. There was also a small dance floor. The DJ was playing garage anthems, and Gina was in her element. They appeared to be a bit drunk already. Lizzy got herself a large glass of Chardonnay and gazed around the bar. As she took in the scenery, her eyes became focused on one particular thing. He was tall, dark hair, tanned and Mediterranean looking. He was also looking over towards Lizzy and gave her the biggest widest smile she had ever seen. It lit the room and she blushed.

Up until this point Lizzy had just wanted to go home. She was fed up with the weather and fed up with the company she was in. The girls were a laugh but she had not expected the holiday to be so dull. Although she loved drinking and partying, she had decided that she was not a party every night girl. She liked to find out about cultures and take in the country she was in.

Lizzy turned around to see Trish and Gina, wiggling their hips to the music that was playing. Shelley was chatting away to Gemma. Just as Lizzy was about to interrupt their conversation, she felt a tap on her shoulder. She turned around to see that the tall dark haired man was right beside her.

"Hola Senorita! Que Tal?" he asked.

Lizzy was stunned. He was absolutely drop dead gorgeous. Lizzy wanted to try and impress him, but her Spanish had gone out of the window.

"Buenos Noches, Senor. Moy bien por favor et tu?" said Lizzy somewhat reluctantly.

Now she wished she had spoken English as he rattled off even more Spanish. He could see that Lizzy was a bit confused.

"My name is Jose, what is your name beautiful Senorita?"

Jose held out is hand to shake Lizzy's hand, but instead he took her hand and kissed is gently. In a daze, Lizzy told him her name and explained that she was from London. Jose owned a small restaurant in the centre of town. He was 30, muscular and very very sexy indeed. Lizzy was all starry eyed, but was soon interrupted by Gina.

"Hello then, who is this?" Gina questioned. Lizzy done the introduction and Jose did not really appear interested in having a conversation with Gina, or any of the other girls.

In true women style, Gina, Trish, Shelley and Gemma all congregated around each other talking about Jose. Whispering to each other and giggling. Lizzy knew exactly what they were saying and felt quite good about the fact that he wanted to speak with her only. She listened intensively to Jose and done the polite yes and no thing without giving too much away about herself. He was indeed very sexy and very Spanish. As the wine started to kick into her brain, she was finding it difficult to actually understand what he was talking about and then promptly got bored. She dismissed herself from the conversation to return to her friends, but made sure that she made a date with him for the following evening.

Gina was still giggling about Jose as they walked back to the apartments.

"Well at least he has not pissed on me!" Stated Lizzy and they all roared with laughter.

Lizzy still wanted to go home. She was missing her daughter and missing the gym. She could not swim in Spain as the weather was so bad, and the   nearest pool was an outdoor pool. It was also closed as the season had not begun yet. Swimming in cold weather had not bothered her. When she stayed in America she had swam naked in the villa pool. It was not heated and very cold, but the water swishing around her body had made her feel good. That was the other thing about swimming. Having the water flowing around her curves. At the apartments, the drink was flowing. Lizzy felt a disconnection from the group. She did not feel like she actually fitted within this group. Although Shelley was her mate, she had also felt the disconnection from her after the sex scenario in the bedroom. She wanted to dismiss this feeling and listened as they all chuckled together and spoke pure drunken nonsense. Lizzy had to admit that it was funny and began to get involved with the conversations.

"Let's go clubbing girls. We can't sit in here all night". Trish was getting unsettled. Lizzy looked at her watch to see that it was 3.30am and decided that she was not going out now.

She knew she could do with a good uninterrupted sleep.

"I'm not going. I am going to get some sleep. You girl's go. Go on don' let me stop you". Lizzy said hoping that they would all disappear for the evening.

Gina, Gemma, Trish and Shelley clinked their glasses together, downed their drinks and left the apartment.

Lizzy was glad of a bit of time on her own. She was not used to having people around her for so long. She liked her own company and liked to sit and be peaceful. She knew that she was on holiday and should be out on the town with the rest of them, but just did not want to go out. She never did anything unless she was happy to do so. She cleared the drinks from the table, washed the glasses and jumped in the shower. The hot water pulsated over her body and she felt a tingle all over. That was one good thing about the apartment. It had a new fitted shower that was very powerful. Some places you stay in, you are lucky whether you get a trickle out of the showerhead. This head was forceful. Any negative thoughts she was feeling started to drift away. She was happy to be away. She was   happy to have met the girls.

She was happy that she had decided to meet Jose the next evening. She was not happy that he had invited all of them. Perhaps it is for the best, she thought to herself. She should not go alone, in a foreign country to meet a foreign bloke in his hometown. That could be potentially dangerous.

She dried herself and moisturised all over. She always moisturised her skin after every shower or bath. She was proud of her skin. It was taught and as soft as silk. Any man who had the good fortune to get close to her always commented on it. Men liked good skin; especially soft skin and she made a point of looking after it. She put on a t-shirt and climbed into the bed. As she lay there she hoped that no one decided to bring back any fellas for sex. She could not cope with that again. Perhaps she was jealous that she was not getting any. That's pathetic, she said to herself.

It did not seem like she had been asleep for long when she was woken by Shelley literally falling through the bedroom door and landing with a thud on the floor. She was laughing loud to herself and shouting out Lizzy's name.

Lizzy woke with a start and jumped up. Shelley was trying to get up, and kept falling back down. She thought that it was very funny. Lizzy was not amused; she was looking forward to sleeping until the morning. However, she got out of her bed to help Shelley get up. As she lifted Shelley from the ground, the pair of them ended up back on the floor. Lizzy was now laughing at the thought of the site of them. Eventually she did get Shelley up and onto the bed. As soon as she lay on the bed, Shelley passed out.

The next morning Shelley woke with a thumping headache. Lizzy gave her a resolve and they conversed about the club she had gone to. She informed Lizzy that they had seen Jose in the club with a woman. Lizzy did not really want to hear the rest of the conversation but still made Shelley confirm what she had seen.

"He had his tongue down her throat mate! Shelley had

explained. His hands were all over her. They then disappeared. "

What a bummer, Lizzy had thought. But what did she really expect. Never mind, she would not be going to meet him later. That she did know.

"Are you up for some breakfast soon Shelley? I am rather peckish" questioned Lizzy.

With that Shelley jumped out of the bed, rushed to the toilet and all Lizzy could here was her heaving. After a few minutes, Shelley returned to the bedroom, laughing loudly, and declared how much money she had wasted by throwing up.

Lizzy decided to get her suitcase in order. They had been there almost a week and she was eager to get home. Their flight was booked for late that night. One last drunken rampage would be on the cards and she did not want to forget anything. She also wanted to get a souvenir for her daughter. She was not going to break the bank but wanted something for her. Her daughter collected key rings and little gadgets, so she would have breakfast and then have a wander about. The weather had really picked up and it was fairly warm. She was excited about the fact that she may even be able to sun bath today.

Gemma, Gina and Trish were up and about. Gina would not let anyone sleep past 9 am. It did not matter how much she drank her how late she was out, she was up, bright and breezy every morning. Lizzy was sick of full English. It was all they had eaten since being in Spain. She wanted something different this morning and opted for a continental breakfast. When the waiter had bought it to her table, she had wished that she had ordered the full English.

It was very pleasant and she had enjoyed it. She decided that she had made the right choice after all. Shelley was still pissed and decided to go for a hair of the dog. Just the thought of that made Lizzy feel ill. She never understood how people could drink to that excess and not throw up all over again.

"Don't knock it until you have tried it!" Shelley laughed as she saw the look on Lizzy's face.

The sun was shining and it was around 70 degrees. Now Lizzy was happy. She could finally get some of the Mediterranean sun she had been hoping for. She suffered with SAD. Seasonal adjustment disorder. She hated the winter, and hated being cold. She had told herself that one-day she would live in a warm country. The sun lifted her spirits and she always felt good in the spring and summer. She did not mind autumn, as it was normally still bright. But winter, she hated it with a vengeance. All five girls were now happy all due to the fact that the sun was shining.

Chapter 10

It had been a long week and Lizzy was so glad to be home. She had a pile of letters stacked in the hallway. Most of them junk mail. She liked junk mail. Sometimes she would find a great bargain, and she loved a bargain. There was also a copy of the local rag.

Fortunately, she had picked up a bottle of milk from the petrol station, on the way back from the airport. She was tired, but fairly refreshed. The little bit of sun she received had given her a small glow to her skin. She knew she would be straight to the sun bed shop as soon as it opened. The birds were signing and it was still dark outside. She made a cup of tea and unpacked her case. She threw a dark wash into the washing machine. Yes the pissed on jeans had to be washed first. Luckily she had packed them away inside a carrier bag so that the rest of her case was not heaving with the smell. She sat at the kitchen table and opened her mail. Bills and more bills and junk mail. She opened the local rag and flicked through the pages. She stopped at the section called Two's company, and scanned through the advertisements. This section had always intrigued Lizzy and she often wondered how sad these people must be. Yet her life was a mess. She was successful, intelligent with good friends, but no lover. All of her friends had slowly but surely hooked up with a guy and she was seeing less and less of them. She was sick of being stuck in of a weekend. Two weekends on a row was enough for her. She wanted some fun. She had thought that the girlie holiday would be fun. But to her disappointment it was not as fun as she had hoped. She read the headings and laughed to herself. Women for women, men for women. , men for men, and good friends. She left the paper on the table as she finished her tea, and then run a bath.

She had felt dirty   with the flying. It always made

her feel dirty. Probably because of the perfuse sweat she endured on every flight. She laid in the bath, shoulders under the water and chilled out. All the time thinking about what she had endured on the holiday. Whilst thinking about the soldier pissing on her and the sex orgies, she knew in her hearts of hearts that her next holiday would not be with the four girls she went with. In fact she had made her mind up that she was never going on a girlie holiday again. She would pretend that she had a fantastic time to all that asked her. She would rave on about the clubs she never really liked much apart from Black and White, and that was short lived due to Shelley disappearing act. Yes her next holiday would definitely be either with her daughter (so she was not subject to the orgies) or with her new man. Well the one she was going to find. Soon.

She emerged out of the bath water, dried herself and covered her body in moisturiser. It was now 8.30am and she felt like she needed to have a sleep. Lizzy was not one for sleeping. She was always worried that if she slept after a flight, that she would miss the day ahead. She had been travelling most of the night, and was feeling tired. Instead she headed out to the sun bed shop for a session of tanning.

On her return, she noticed the local rag, still on the same page, lying on the kitchen table. She picked it up and read one of the ads, under the men for women column. 6ft tall, brown hair/eyes, very loving caring and reliable. Looking for someone special. There was a telephone number at the end of the column. Hmm. She thought to herself. To her own amazement she picked up the phone and dialled the customer services number.

"Two's Company Can I help you?" said the operator.

"Yes" said Lizzy rather confidently. *"I wish to place an ad."*

"OK what section would you like to place the ad, and do you know what you would like to say as we have our own pre written ads" replied the operator.

"I have my own wording thanks. I want to

place it under the women for men section please" said a nervous Lizzy. And she rattled of her ad to the operator. The operator repeated what Lizzy had told her and explained that the ad could take up to two weeks to be published. The ad was free and Lizzy had a special pass code to access her messages.

At the end of the conversation, Lizzy wrote the pass code and the telephone number on a piece of paper and pinned it to her notice board in the kitchen. She then threw the paper in the bin. It took a few minutes to sink in what she had done, and then had a sheer panic. *Oh my God does that make me as sad as the other people placing ads. No, remember you just want to go out and have fun.* She dismissed any negative thoughts as she reminded herself that she was not a sad case, but wanted to try something different. She was not looking for love or the man of her dreams, her knight in shining armour, she was looking for fun and that was exactly the attitude that she was going to take.

With a spring in her step, she became excited about the prospect that she may meet new people. She liked meeting new people and going to new places. She had become a bit bored with the places she would go with her friends as they were always the same places and consequently you would see the same old faces. She wanted something fresh in her life, and thought that this would be a good way to get that.

She also wondered if she would get any response from her ad. Only time would tell and she was looking forward to finding out. It was also her little secret and she would not tell anyone. Well not until she needed to. She knew her daughter would have a blind fit, and her friends would think that she had completely lost the plot. Lizzy did not care what any of them thought. Placing the ad was going to change her life.

Chapter 11

For the past two weeks Lizzy had been stuck in her humdrum life of going to work, going to the gym, and listening to her mates constantly talking about their new or existing guys in their life. She had not seen Kai at the gym at all. She was not really expecting to see him, as she had been going after work. She had met him in the day and subsequently had dismissed any romance with him. She was contemplating going to the club he had suggested on Friday night. He had told Lizzy that every three weeks he would go there with his friends, and this would be the 3rd week. She did not particularly like this club. It was an over 35 crowd. Which was cool in her book, but the music they played was awful. She hated the fact that all the clubs that catered for the older crowd seemed to think that they did not like the same music as the younger crowds. Lizzy loved music, not the Abba crap that these places always played. Why do they do that? She had been to this club once, with her friend Sam and Sam's friend 'the bitch ', actually her name was Cila. It was Cila's birthday and Lizzy spent the whole night drinking wine and watching the so obvious married men trying to pull anything in a skirt for a Friday night shag. She could only describe it as being a meat market. Cila had liked it there. This was a woman who was so up her own arse it was unbelievable. She was fake and full of pretence. Sam seemed to like her but Lizzy was not keen at all. The more time Lizzy spent with her the more she did not like her. She was not a genuine person at all, but just out for herself. Lizzy did not like that in people so consequently, did not go out with her after that night. Anytime Sam mentioned that Cila may be coming along on a night out, she made up an excuse not to go. Lizzy had told Sam exactly what she thought of her. Lizzy could speak with Sam about anything and anyone. She was truly her best buddy and had a lot of respect for her. Even though she did not like the wanker she was living with. Lizzy never held back on her thoughts with that either. She had blatantly told   Sam what she had thought of him and blatantly told him that he was not good enough for her. Four years on and they are still together. Lizzy knew it would not last much longer, there were large unsealable cracks emerging in the relationship.

Luke had not stopped going on about the holiday and thought that he knew everything that Lizzy must have gotten up to. If only he had known the truth! She just went along with it. He was still as sexy as ever, but she kept him in the look but don't touch category. Every day at work, she would glance at him on the sly, whilst he pranced around the office, trying out his new chat up lines on the young girls. Lizzy was a bit passed all of that. She liked a good conversation and would talk to a man for hours, if he were interesting. As soon as they started the chat up lines, she would lose interest immediately. She found them corny, cheesy and irritating. Don't get me wrong, Lizzy liked a bit of flattery. It made her feel good. But too much of the gift of the gab became annoying. It's like they rehearse it and have nothing else to talk about. Ask them a question in mid-stream and they become flustered and then talk even more shit. She liked a man with a brain. Someone who knew how to please a women with intelligent conversation. That is where she connected. If a man could connect with her brain, as well as physically, she would be turned on for longer than an everlasting light bulb.

She was still unsure about going to the club. She did want to see Kai. He had all of the attributes she liked. He was intelligent, charming and had good manners. He also made her feel attractive. He was not really her type to look at. Then she did not really have a type. Actually she did have a type. The Vin Diesel type. He was her ideal man. To look at anyway. But she had no chance getting hold of Vin. Long distance relationships don't work anyway!

After a hard day at work, she returned home and found the local rag sitting in her hallway. She threw down her bag and went straight to the two's company pages. There it was. Staring her right in her face. Her advertisement. Under the women for men section it read;

Intelligent, solvent, sexual female, GSOH, 37, seeks genuine, solvent male to share fun nights out with. Only sincere people need apply.

Her advertisement had finally been printed and she was excited. She was also a bit apprehensive and started to doubt her own integrity. She passed it off again as a bit of fun. What harm could it do? Although the paper was her local rag, it was distributed as far as Southend. She had seen the ad's regularly. There were definitely people out there that were having fun using this method of dating. She had also heard some terror stories whereby people have been stalked, raped and even killed. She did not like the thought of that at all and new that she would have to be very very careful. She also knew that if she did go to meet anyone, she would have to tell one of her mates. She would confide in Sam. When the time was right.

She was itching to call her number to see if anyone had left any messages, but decided to hold on for a couple of days, until the paper had been distributed to all its destinations. She read the ad over and over and wondered if it did reflect her as a person. She knew that it was a bit late in the day to try and change what she had written, and let go of any further thoughts regarding it. She was scared, yet also relishing the act of meeting new guys.

After three days of containment, she decided to ring the number. She was very nervous as she dialled the number and her palms were sweating. Before she dialled the last digit, she put the phone down and poured a glass of wine. She sat at the kitchen table with a pen and a pad, so that she could jot down anything that had interested her. After taking a large gulp of the wine, for Dutch courage, she redialled the number and was told to tap in her pass code using the keypad of the phone. She was slightly shaking. The automated voice on the other end of the receiver stated that Lizzy had 35 messages. *Wow!* She thought to herself, and hurriedly pushed the keypad to receive the first of the messages. All of the guys described themselves, their height weight and what they liked doing. Lizzy first listened to the voice to see if she found that to be sexy, and then wrote down the stats of each. As she reached the last message, her daughter walked in to the kitchen.

"Mum, you have been on the phone for ages, what are you doing? I want to phone my friend Sharon"

Lizzy panicked slightly and told her daughter that she would not be long, but it was too late she was already reading the notes that Lizzy had been making. She gave Lizzy a puzzled look and after Lizzy had put the phone down her daughter started to ask her lots of questions.

Lizzy explained that she was bored with her life and wanted to meet new people. She explained about the ad and that she had 35 callers whom wanted to meet up with her. It was just a bit of fun, she tried to assure her daughter, who by this point was totally disgusted with her mother's actions. No harm will come from it; it's a laugh. Lizzy daughter knew she was a bit of a wild one. Lizzy also knew with a bit of understanding she would come around to the idea. Lizzy filled up her wine glass and then read through her notes, crossing off anyone that she did not like the sound of. She was left with ten prospective dates. They had all left a contact number and she decided that she would ring each one and ask them a set of questions.

Question one, why did you reply to my ad. What was it about my ad that attracted you to call me? Lizzy felt like she was interviewing for a new recruit. She wanted to be careful, and knew that this would be the best way forward.

Question two, tell me about yourself. What do you like doing and why.

Question three. What is your occupation? She liked this one. It would let her know if they were solvent and responsible.

Question four. What were you hoping to gain from meeting me?

Lizzy would know by the reply to question two as to whether she would meet any one of the guys. She would also know from the initial greeting. If she did not like his voice then she would not like him. She also knew that she should not be so judgmental. After all said and done, she had placed the ad.

She dismissed the first 5 calls, as she did not like the sound of them at all. Her 6th call was a man called Stuart. He was 6ft tall with dark brown hair. She definitely had a thing for height. He was also a policeman. He liked clubbing and cooking. He also liked walking and romantic picnics. His job had restricted him from meeting a woman and he saw the ad and thought that he would also like some fun. Lizzy arranged to meet him. Tuesday, 8pm in the Wishing Well Pub in Chingford.

The 7th call was a man called Monty. He was 5ft 11, dark hair and Italian. He lived in Romford. He had his own flat and a young daughter. He was a chef and very confident He had a very sexy voice and Lizzy arranged to meet him on Saturday at 9pm.

The 8th call was a man called Simon. He had a young daughter and lived in Southend. Lizzy arranged to meet him at 6.30pm on Saturday.

The 9th call was a man named Mick. He was blonde, 6ft tall, medium build and sounded like he had his feet firmly on the ground. Lizzy arranged to meet him the following Friday night at the Dog and Duck in Walthamstow at 8pm.

The last man had two daughters. He had a Victorian house in Romford and had been divorced for a year. He was ready for fun and Lizzy arranged to meet him on Monday @ 8.30pm in O'Neal's in Ilford.

With all of these dates in her diary, she was going to be a busy girl over the next week or so. How exciting, she thought to herself. This is going to be fun, fun, and fun.

By the end of the calls, Lizzy had polished off a bottle of wine and felt slightly intoxicated. She was no longer thinking about going to meet Kai, and Luke was nowhere to be found in her mind. She had lined herself up with 5 dates and was ready to disclose all to her best friend Sam.

Chapter 12

It was Tuesday already and Lizzy had not confided in Sam as of yet. She knew she should call and explain just in case she needed a get out clause. Luke was hovering around her desk and she was desperate for him to leave so that she called call Sam at work. It was past lunchtime and she did not have much time left. Sam was going to have a blue fit once she told her what she had done, but she knew that she would understand. Lizzy was also certain that Sam would not let her down. Stuart was her first date. The policeman. She kept fantasying about him in his uniform and that was the real attraction for her. She loved a uniform, especially a coppers uniform. Like most women the thought of this was a complete turn on, along with fire man and soldiers. Soldiers were a different breed though. She had dated a soldier, but needless to say it did not last long. He was too interested as to whether she had done the housework for his return, than in her. Hmm. She thought.

Luke was still hovering and she decided to find out exactly why he was.

"Luke what is it. I'm busy?" said an aggravated Lizzy.

"Well Lizzy" said Luke looking rather awkward. "I thought that maybe we could go out for a drink after work?"

"Who's going?" questioned Lizzy.

"Well I thought perhaps, just you and me?"

Great! Lizzy thought. All these months of drawling over this bloke, and the fact that she had put herself in denial, and now he wants to know, when she already had a bloody date.

"Sorry, Luke, maybe another time. I already have plans." She dismissed him from her   desk

With that he walked away and this was now the perfect time for her to call Sam.

"Sam, Hi its Lizzy can you talk?" questioned Lizzy.

"I'm a bit busy babe, what's up" said Sam, coming across somewhat hassled.

Well, I have a date tonight and I am meeting him at 8pm at the Wishing Well. I need for you to call me around 9.00, in case I need to make excuses to leave" explained Lizzy.

"Why an earth would you need to make excuses. Who is he? You never mentioned this before" said a now puzzled Sam.

"I know, I put an ad in the paper and I have lined up 5 dates. I need you to help me out, as I don't know who they are. But I am meeting the first one tonight. He is a copper, it should be OK and I have arranged the meetings in public places".

Lizzy had started to realise how strange this whole scenario was as she heard herself confess all to Sam.

"For crying out loud girl, what were you thinking?" Sam was in a blind panic. She had known Lizzy since she was 5 and knew that she was a bit of a girl, but never thought that she would do something like this.

"Honestly, Sam, It will be fine. Please say you will call me" begged Lizzy.

Lizzy could rely on Sam. She knew that she would call her and she knew that she would get the Spanish inquisition later.

As she replaced the receiver, she felt better about the date. She wondered if he was what he said he was. As the afternoon ticked on, Lizzy sat pondering on what to wear. Being a weekday, she would opt for her jeans and a nice top. She would have to wear a jacket, as it was still chilly. The summer had not hit the lovely town of Walthamstow as of yet, and she was relishing the day that it would. She could sit in the garden, at the weekends, in her Bikini, giving the neighbours the shock of their lives, again.

She did not live far from the pub and would drive there. It would only take around 15 minutes. She would have plenty of time as she left work early. It normally took her an hour to get home on the train. How she hated the train. She hated travelling to and from work. It was a complete nightmare. Especially, in the summer months. Some dirty stinking arm pit, would be thrust into your face in the rush hour. Failing that you were guaranteed to get someone's disgusting garlic breath right by your head first thing in the morning. Some people have no consideration!

Stuart the policeman! Lizzy was excited and also nervous. As she got herself ready, she began to sweat. She sprayed a bit more of her Eternity perfume behind her ears and left the house.

She parked the car and was unsure whether she actually wanted to go inside. She had spoken to Stuart and he had told her that he would be wearing a black top and dark blue jeans. He should be easy enough to spot, she had thought, as he was 6ft. She plucked up the courage and walked into the bar. As she did, it seemed like everyone had turned around to watch her entrance, which made her feel even more nervous. Stuart was standing by a table next to the entrance. He walked straight over to her and asked if her name was Lizzy. She looked up at him (she had put her flats on) and he had lovely big brown eyes. He also had a rather large nose and a protruding chin. He was not a very handsome looking man at all. He ordered her a glass of Chardonnay and they sat at the table and discussed their lives, what they like, what they dislike. All Lizzy kept thinking was what he looked like in his uniform.

9.00 on the dot and Lizzy's mobile was ringing. It was Sam.

"Liz, you alright? Are you still with the copper? What's he like? Can you call me in a while so I know that you are OK?" said

Sam with sheer panic in her voice.

"Hi, Yes, I'm in a bar in Chingford. I'll be home soon; can I call you back then?"

Lizzy was trying to be cool as Sam was bombarding her with questions. She felt like a little school kid being asked questions by her mother. She did not want the copper to know she had someone checking up on her welfare. After all, it was none of his business anyway.

Stuart bought another drink and surprisingly the evening went pleasantly well. He seemed kind, considerate and even funny. He did have a good sense of humour and Lizzy liked that in a man. He asked if he could call her and she agreed.

On the way home, Lizzy thought about Luke and was glad that she had not gone out for a drink with him. She knew that after a glass or two of Chardonnay she would no doubt have tried to play tonsil tennis and then regret it the next morning. However, Luke was outstandingly sexy. One taste of his sugar and Lizzy would want more. That's why she kept her distance from him. He was like the forbidden fruit.

As soon as Lizzy entered the house she called Sam to assure her that she was OK. She thanked her for the prompt call and said she would speak with her in the next few days. She had a few more calls that she would need her to make and she would let her know when these would be. As she put the phone down on Sam, she was not expecting her mobile to ring at that moment. It was Stuart.

"Hi, Liz, I had a great night. How about we meet on Saturday. We could go out for a meal or may be a club. I have that weekend off" said Stuart.

He is a fast mover, thought Lizzy.

"Can't do it this weekend Stuart, I have plans. How about the following week some time". Lizzy had plans alright.

She was meeting two guys in one evening. She had not mentioned to Stuart that she had arranged to meet 4 other guys. If he did not know then he must be stupid. Then it dawned on her that he might think that she had chosen him only. She dismissed even thinking about what he thought, as she did not really care. She was not going to get attached to any one and this was supposed to be fun for her. That is exactly the way she was going to make it. They did agree to catch up by phone in the week and arrange another date. Lizzy's mind was already moving on to the next fella she was going to meet at the weekend.

Chapter 13

It had been a funny old week and once again, Lizzy was at the Friday night scenario, with no one to go out with. She had two dates on Saturday and was happy with that. She was pissed off with drinking by herself and decided to have an early night.

The following morning she woke up around 10 am, which was rather late for Lizzy. She had worked hard and felt slightly stressed. She hated that stress feeling as it messed with her mind. Clarity of thought was what she needed now and headed out to the gym for her usual swim, steam and Jacuzzi. She had increased her lengths now to 40 and was rather chuffed with herself. It did not take her any longer and she had made good progress. The first 6 lengths were always the hardest and after the initial pain in her arms had eased she could swim like a dolphin. She could not seem to think straight this morning but did not know what was bothering her.

The Jacuzzi was empty and Lizzy emerged herself into the warm water. Instead of turning on the jets, she held onto the side and let her body float. She could feel the stress lifting from her body and she went into a small state of meditation. Just as she was about to go deeper, she heard a voice. A voice she knew, but could not remember who it belonged to.

"Hey Lizzy, I thought someone was dead in the Jacuzzi then, what are you doing? "said Kai.

As she turned around, to her delight, there was Kai. She had not thought too much about Kai, as she had not seen him for weeks. She felt a tingle through her body as he sat next to her in the Jacuzzi. She was really pleased to see him.

"Where have you been stranger? I have not seen you for ages?" he questioned.

Kai explained that he had been busy and had also taken his daughter away for a few days. His eyes were sparkling and he had a beautiful smile. Lizzy had indeed forgotten how nice he actually was. As they chatted away, their legs kept brushing against each other in the warm water, as they appeared to sit closer and closer to each other. The jets were now on and no one else could see. Twice Lizzy's leg brushed against his and she apologised, as she felt embarrassed. He did not seem to mind at all and did not even acknowledge that she had touched his leg or apologised for it.

"I've been meaning to catch up with you Lizzy. I have a bit of a dilemma going on and I am not sure how to deal with it" he declared.

Lizzy felt good that he wanted to confide in her and the suspense was killing her. It must be a business issue, or something to do with the cooking contracts, she had flattered herself with these thoughts. But then, her bubble burst as he started to talk all about a women that he really liked and went on to describe details of the situation he had somehow found himself in.

Lizzy ego was rather deflated by this, as she was sure that they had a spark going on between themselves. Had she misread the signs? Were there ever any signs? Did she make it all up in her own mind to satisfy the sub conscious wanting of a man? What an earth was going on here? She felt stupid. She withheld any type of emotion as she listened to his carry on's and then advised him accordingly. He also stated how he did not want a relationship this year, at all, but wanted to make sure he had the time for his daughter, who was doing her GCSE's. He liked Lizzy advice and then out of nowhere she spun a little web of her own. She told Kai how she had met a guy, whom she did like, but understood his need for singledom and a non-committed relationships. She told how this guy had been ringing her constantly and she had to tell him to back off a bit. Who was she kidding? If only that was the case. They laughed together at the prospect of unwanted texts and phone calls. Lizzy felt better now that she had invented this person, but still wondered how and why she could have misread the signals.

She left the gym, knowing that was the end of any affair she had going on in her head. She actually felt disgusted with herself. Well at least she had the dates later.

She quite liked the idea of Monty, the Italian. She was not meeting him until 9pm and had rearranged the meeting with Simon. She was originally due to meet him in Southend at 6.30pm. She was not sure if it would give her enough time. She had spoken with Simon the night before to finalise details. He had a higher pitched voice than she could remember and was a bit dubious about meeting him. Gina lived in Southend and she had contacted her to arrange to meet with her after the date. It would also give Lizzy somewhere to freshen up, prior to meeting Monty in Romford. Lizzy had also called Monty the night before to confirm details. In each case she had made a point that if they were not about to turn up to the meeting that they should have the decency to call her. It was common courtesy and although she did not know these people, she expected to be treated with common courtesy.

She was still pissed off about the conversation that she had with Kai. Unless, she thought to herself, he was sounding her out. Yet no numbers had been exchanged and she was not going to give her number to him so easily. She wanted to. He seemed like a pleasant bloke and could do with a new mate. After all, she was not expecting to find the love of her life through dating people from the paper. What she had not anticipated was what was to come.

Driving to Southend Lizzy had the music blaring and was chain smoking. She often chain smoked when she was nervous. Today she was nervous. She had a funny feeling about Simon. She did not know what it was or why she had felt this way and that concerned her. Lizzy, generally, was a laid back person. She took life's ups and down's on the chin and always dusted off and got back up again. She had a change of clothes in her boot and Valentino perfume in her handbag. Every now and again she sprayed a little on her clothes, to try and get rid of the ashtray smell she had adopted from the chain smoking. Why did she smoke? She had often asked that question. She did not like it, it done nothing for her and she was paranoid of the smell of it. Hence, she spent a fortune on perfumes. Lizzy would not buy the cheap stuff. All of her perfumes cost over £30 for a small 30ml bottle. Her handbag invariably was also well stocked with chewing gums and mints. Well you never know when you need that just brushed your teeth smell! She would have to try and stop smoking. She really wanted to, but always put it off. Why she put it off she did not know. Perhaps it was the fear of withdrawal pangs. She had heard that coming off of nicotine was the same as coming off of heroine. That scared the shit out of her.

As she pulled into the Bell car park, off the A127, she called Simon to find out if he was there. He was. He was waiting at the entrance. Lizzy could not see the entrance directly, but could see a person in the distance. She parked the car, sprayed again, shoved a chewing gum in her mouth and then proceeded to the front of the pub. She could see a man, around 5ft 11, dark hair, glasses and with a large round belly. He was also dressed as if he were in his 50's. Lizzy looked at Simon, and could not believe what she had met up with. He was like the bogey boy in school. He was indeed Lizzy's worst nightmare. However, she decided not to be so shallow.

"Hi Simon, I can't stop long. I have to go to my mate's house. She invited me for dinner. It's her kid's birthday. Just one drink eh?" said Lizzy.

Lizzy felt bad, but knew it was the right thing to do.

His voice now appeared even higher than before and Lizzy did not like this meeting at all. He was dull, dreary, with no charm. He lived with his mum. Lizzy hated men that lived with their mum. To her it meant that they couldn't fend by themselves. Mum running behind them and picking up their dirty washing. Lizzy knew that men wanted a mother figure really, and she was determined not to go down that route. She had been there and done that, and vowed never to do it again. The only reason these men wanted a girlfriend was because they could not fuck their mothers. Harsh she thought, but so true. Simon was also spotty and his conversation was boring. Lizzy sat in the pub with this geek, thinking that if this was the type of person replying or place ads, then she had no hope. She certainly was not in the league of bogey boy Simon and she certainly was not desperate. She needed to get out of there and fast. Simon had sensed her anguish.

Lizzy picked up her mobile phone and rudely made a call. She excused herself from the meeting. Her excuse, late for dinner and had to dash. Simon did not look very pleased, but Lizzy really did not give a shit. He had had far too much of her time already. Her time was precious and she was not one to give it away easily. She started to think that maybe this dating was a bad idea.

When she reached Gina's, she could not contain the sheer amusement of the whole scenario and shared her jokes with Gina. Gina said that she admired Lizzy for even going into the pub. Gina said that if she had seen this fella she would have made excuses instantly. Lizzy was not like that. She liked to give people a chance, as sometimes, well almost never, the first impression may be wrong. In this case it was 100% correct.

She had a bite to eat. Gina's kids were at their friends. There was no birthday. Lizzy made that up. She freshened up and changed her top. She was supposed to meet Monty at 9pm in Romford. As she approached the A12, she decided to give him a quick call.

"Monty, hi, it's Lizzy. What was the name of the place we were meeting at?" asked Lizzy.

"Liz, sorry, I cannot meet you. The babysitter has let me down. You could come to my flat if you like?" Monty said with no assurance in his voice.

Great! Lizzy thought. What a flipping day this is turning out to be.

"Ok, I'm on the A12 just approaching Romford. Where do you live?" asked Lizzy.

"Ah, maybe you shouldn't come here. I mean I don't know you, you could be a psycho?" he said.

After the date Lizzy had already had, she did not need this shit.

"Look, it's up to you. I can just as easy carry on driving" she stated quite sternly.

Monty gave Lizzy the address and it was not long before she was outside his flat.

His flat was part of a block and they seemed well maintained. She pressed the buzzer for number 20. Monty answered and let her in.

Monty was one of the more promising dates to Lizzy. They had talked a few times on the phone and appeared to get on well. He said he was Italian and 5ft 11. He also said that he was stocky built. Lizzy liked the stocky look. As long as it was not fat but toned.

As she approached the door ready to knock, it opened. There stood Monty. He was a handsome chap, with dark brown eyes and dark brown hair. He showed her to the living room where he had been sitting drinking a Bud.

"Where is your daughter?" Lizzy said looking around, half expecting to see a toddler running around.

"Bed, do you wanna drink?" he asked.

"Nah ta, so tell me about you" Lizzy said cutting to the chase.

Lizzy could see that Monty was not comfortable with her being there. This may have been due to the fact that he was actually around 5ft 5 and skinny. He did not look Italian either. Why do people lie? she thought to herself. Why? You are what you are. People either like you or they don't. That was Lizzy's philosophy. It worked for her. She never lied about anything. Well apart from the incident with Simon, but that was different.

They had small talk for around 10 minutes, but Lizzy had lost interest in Monty almost instantly. As a gesture of good will she allowed him that 10 minutes of her time and then, once again, made excuses to leave.

"Monty, sorry I have to leave. My daughter is due home soon and I don't like to leave her in the house on her own". Liar, liar. At this rate, Lizzy would be adopting a new friend. A great big nose from all the lies she had told today. However, they were all justified lies and she was happy with the outcome.

Driving home she once again wondered if she had done the right thing by placing this ad. She could hear her phone ringing. It was Stuart.

"Hey Liz, how did the date go?" asked Stuart.

"What date?" said an astonished Lizzy. She knew she had not told him.

"The one you had today. Come on its Saturday night and you're trying to tell me you blew me out to go out with the girls? So come on, how did it go?"

Lizzy had enough of lies for one day and proceeded to tell Stuart all about her day. He found it highly amusing and they laughed together at her misfortunes. It was not long and she was home. Her conversation with Stuart had ended and she just wanted to go to bed. She was deflated and pissed off at the amount of time she had wasted. She called Sam and told her everything.

Sam also laughed at her misfortunes. She had two more dates lined up for the following week. She was not sure if she was going to go. She was not sure that she had not become a sad bastard with no life. Just as she was about to go to sleep, her mobile rung again.

"Hey Liz, its Stuart. I've booked a table for us for next Tuesday. It's an Indian restaurant. You do like Indian don't you?" asked Stuart.

This man was becoming persistent. That intrigued her but also annoyed her. She agreed on the date and put the phone down. So far, Stuart had been about the only sane one she had met. She did not fancy him at all. In her mind, his facial appearance was not so kind to the eyes. But hey, it would get her out and he did make her laugh.

Chapter 14

After a hectic week, it was Friday night. This time Lizzy had a date. It had been a good month since she had been out on a Friday night. She was looking forward to it. Her daughter was staying with her Nan. Her daughter loved staying with her Nan. It made her wonder whether she actually wanted to spend any time with her mother at all. Lizzy put it down to her age. It would come to a point when she would not want to stay with her Nan, as she would be clubbing herself. She knew that Nan would not be happy with that one. It sometimes upset Lizzy that she did not seem to spend enough time with her daughter. She loved her dearly. She was also hopeful that things would change, once she was a bit older.

The Dog and Duck was not far from where Lizzy lived and it would only take her 10 minutes to drive there. She was nervous again, but getting used to the blind date scenario. She was hoping that she would not be meeting another minger or short arse that had tried to pretend he was in the same league as Vin Diesel. Once again Sam had her back and would call at a designated time.

Lizzy had trouble finding a spot to park. Apparently, Mick lived in Tottenham, which was also not far from the pub. She walked in and looked around. She could not see any blonde 6ft tall men so she decided to order a drink and sit down at a table near to the entrance. That way she would see him as soon as he walked in. This time though, if she did not like the look of him, she would make a quick exit, without any acknowledgement. As far as Lizzy was concerned, she had wasted enough time.

The door swung open. A blonde guy, with sparkling blue eyes, strolled into the pub. He was wearing a long cashmere coat. Lizzy looked up and he smiled in her direction. He pointed to himself and said his name. It was indeed Mick. Lizzy stood up from the chair and said her name.   He smiled an even bigger smile and asked if she wanted a drink.

He returned to the table with two glasses of wine. Lizzy could not believe her luck. This man was drop dead gorgeous. Happy days! She said to herself. They chatted for a while and he told her how he used to model. She could see why. He was tall, toned and handsome.

"Can we go somewhere else?" Lizzy asked Mick. Before Lizzy even thought about what she had said, she had invited him back to hers for coffee.

As she closed the street door behind them, she found herself connected to him by their lips and tongues exploring each other's mouths. The chemistry was unbelievable and Lizzy's hands were all over his body. God what a body he had. She led him up stairs where they had explosive sex. Firstly on the stairs, then the landing and then the bedroom. It was sex that she had never experienced before. Well, she probably had, but it had been so long that she would have forgotten. He was hot and horny and she was enjoying every minute of it. They were romping as if they would never romp again. This carried on until the early hours of the morning and Lizzy lost count on how many times she had climaxed. This, she thought, is exactly what the doctor had ordered. She was shocked at herself and her behaviour. She did not care for one night stands. But on this occasion she had made an exception. And boy, was she glad she had. It had been a long time since she was thrust into the throes of passion, and this man certainly knew what he was doing when it came to the female counterparts. At one point Lizzy caught her breath, as his manhood thrust deep inside her touching areas that she never knew existed. Where did he get his stamina?

Totally knackered and shagged out Lizzy wanted to sleep. So much so that she asked Mike to leave. He had her number and she just hoped that he would contact her again in the not too distant future. Lizzy was glad it was Saturday, she could stay in bed as long as she wanted. Her sheets smelt of testosterone and it was making her high. God what a night. She smiled widely to herself.

The room was lit by a flash of lightening and then a clap of thunder vibrated against the walls of the house. The rain thrashed down as if it wanted to drown all in its path. Lizzy pulled the testosterone covered quilt around her body and fell asleep.

Lizzy was woken by her mobile phone. It was ringing so loudly that it made her jump. She stretched over to the bed side cabinet and as she answered checked the clock for the time. It was 5.30 p.m. and she had been asleep for most of the day. It was Mike.

"Hey Lizzy, I need to speak with you. It's important. Can I come over later?" asked Mick almost pleading with her.

Lizzy was still sleepy and a touch aggravated. What was so important that he needed to see me tonight? Oh my god, she thought. He has a disease. Shit, Shit, He has given me a dose of something. I'm gonna die a horrible death. Why did I sleep with him? She knew why, he was bloody horny and she had not met someone of that calibre for a long time. She soon calmed down when she remembered they had protected sex. Thanks Christ for that. She had done the sensible thing by making him wear a condom. They had nearly gone bare back, but she was insistent. No harm done there then. "Please Liz". Mike was now begging. She was intrigued and agreed to let him come over.

She got out of bed and showered. Even though she washed vigorously she could still smell him on her skin. The door knocked and she answered to find Mike on the door step half an hour early. They sat in the living room and she gave him a beer.

"What's up Mike?" she asked.

Mike started to pour his little heart out about his life. He was off to Spain today for 3 months and wanted Lizzy to go with him. He had business there. Lizzy was flattered but could not accept his offer. He wanted Lizzy to wait for him. 3 months, he explained was not a long time.

"There's also something else you need to know" he said quite sheepishly.

"I am an ex heroin addict. I don't touch it anymore and I am a counsellor for addicts. I have been clean now for a year. By ex-girlfriend who has my child is also an addict" Mick declared.

Lizzy looked at Mike in complete despair. She could not believe what the man was telling her and at this point was so glad that she had made him use a condom. With complete fear in her eyes, she explained that 3 months was a long time and that she never really knew him. She also explained that although he may be off of the heroin, she could not deal with such issues. With that, he left. Never to be seen again.

Lizzy was gutted. She could not believe that this could happen. Sex with Mike was great. Heroin frightened the life out of her.

She was done with this dating lark. She decided to cancel her Monday night date. She picked up her mobile phone and called the guy in Romford.

"Hi it's Lizzy, got to cancel; I've met someone who I really like. Sorry", and put the phone down. She did not even give him a chance to speak.

One thing was for sure; she was going to the STD clinic 1st thing Monday morning to be checked out. She had to be sure that everything was OK. She knew it was as she had used protection, but to satisfy her own mind, she would go to the clinic anyway.

It was around 8pm and once again her mobile was ringing. *For crying out loud, can't a girl get a bit of piece around here?* She shouted out loud. As she looked at the caller ID she could see that it was the copper. *He picks his moments,* thought

Lizzy.

"Liz, hey what you doing? Fancy coming out for a drink. We are going to a club in Brentwood. My mate is coming" asked Stuart.

"Nah, not tonight, Stuart" said Lizzy.

"Come on babe, it will be fun" he persisted.

Lizzy sat and thought for a minute. If she did not go, what was she going to do? Sit in doors and mope about.

"Will you be able to come and get me Stuart?" she asked.

"I'll be there in 1 hour. Be ready, gorgeous" he said as he put the phone down.

Lizzy put the phone down and decided to have another shower to see if she could get rid of Mike's smell. She put on her glad rags, dried her hair, applied her makeup and was ready to rock and roll.

Fuck men, she thought.

Stuart was right on time. Lizzy was taking a shine to this guy. He was no Adonis, but was funny and kind. That is exactly what she needed right now. As she did not fancy him, she had no fear of having sex. So, with that in mind she prepared herself for a night on the town.

The club was crap, the music was crap, but Stuart and his friend were definitely up for fun. The Vodka and Red bull was flowing and at one point Lizzy had 4 glasses lined up. She thought she was a drinker but these guys were putting her to shame. By the end of the night the three of them were shit faced. Stuart called a cab, and they headed off to his flat. His mate was indeed his flat mate. Lizzy wondered how she was going to get home. A cab from Brentwood would cost her a fortune. She was not prepared to pay that. So instead she asked Stuart if she could kip on his sofa.

Stuart got a blanket and some sheets for Lizzy and made the sofa into a bed. He also gave her a t-shirt to wear. She could just about see as she was so pissed. She had a great night. The guys were really funny. Stuart handed her a glass of wine and sat next to her on the make do bed. She drank the wine and felt very tired. It was not long and she had fallen asleep, only to be woken by Stuart caressing her most intimate parts. Lizzy was not sure how long this had been going on and as she opened her eyes, Stuart started kissing her neck. It felt nice to Lizzy and she was enjoying the sensual touch that he had. She tried not to look at his face, as he was rather an odd one. Instead she lay there and let him carry on with his caresses. She was becoming very moist indeed and was enjoying every moment. Sure, it was different from the night before. That was pure animalistic sex. Raw. This was tender. Lizzy liked both and now that Mike had gone, perhaps, she thought, it was time for something different. It then dawned on her what was going on.

Stuart had now decided to move his action plan one step forward. Under normal circumstances, Lizzy would not have let herself get into this compromising position. She was so drunk that she could barely move. Her head was spinning. It then triggered in her head exactly where he was going with this. She could feel him touching her and it was not what she wanted. Not now, not yet. She could not even speak properly due to the alcohol. With the realisation Lizzy's head started to spin even faster. Before she could help herself, she heaved and puked up all over Stuart. It certainly stopped him in his tracks and he jumped up from the make do bed and looked at Lizzy in complete disgust.

"Sorry, I never meant to"... Heave. And she was off again. This time Stuart had found a bucket to stick under her head. She felt like she had bought up the entire contents of her insides and her stomach lining. She felt rough, really rough. She was not embarrassed at all, which surprised her. She was not bothered that the cream carpet was ruined by her vomit. *Serve's him bloody right, taking advantage of a drunk women,* she thought. She cleaned up what she could and showered. She put her clothes back on.

"I don't suppose you would take me home Stuart?" she asked. Whilst she was in the shower, Stuart had called a cab. He gave her forty quid and waved her goodbye.

On the way home Lizzy had started to have negative thoughts about herself. She hated it when this happened, and sometimes she would really beat herself up. What an earth was she playing at? Lady you need to get a grip. Lizzy paid the cab and still had a score change. What a result she thought. She went upstairs and climbed straight into bed. This time she needed to sleep off the alcohol and hopefully forget about ugly bollocks trying to fuck her. She was really angry with herself. Then she thought that she wouldn't have minded if he had put the uniform on, but all she could think about was his huge nose and protruding chin. So what that he made you laugh, she thought. Jokes on you know girl. How could you let that ugly fucker touch you? Let's just say that he looked alright once the beer goggles were on. That's it blame the drink. Blame something, but don't blame yourself. With those thoughts in her mind she passed out on the bed.

Chapter 15

Funny thing was, even though she had completely slated him in her own mind, Lizzy continued to see Stuart. He was indeed funny, and every time she was with him, she would have a great time. They went to the movies, out for drinks, dinner with his friends and she was really enjoying herself. It had come to the point where she had willingly slept with him. He was pretty mediocre in the bedroom department and she could not persuade him to wear his uniform. She liked the thought of dating a copper. It made her feel safe. The more time she spent with him the more she liked him. Although she always made sure she had drunk a few glasses of wine before sleeping with him. Actually it was more like a bottle. She knew in her subconscious that he was not right for her. But for some unknown reason, she continued in the relationship, to the extent that they booked a holiday to Cyprus.

It was a Friday night and she was waiting for Stuart to arrive. They were going to drink locally and then pop into the local nightclub. As she was getting ready the phone rang. It was Jenny and she was in tears. Lizzy could not understand what she was blabbering on about and told her to get ready, come to hers and then they could talk. Jenny agreed and put the phone down. At this point Lizzy was not bothered that Stuart was coming over. She needed to console her mate. In fact Lizzy had known Jenny for a couple of years and had never known her to be upset over anything. Angry maybe, but not to cry.

Lizzy opened a bottle of Chardonnay, poured a glass for herself and then got dressed. As she was applying her make up the doorbell rang and Jenny had arrived in a cab. Lizzy handed her a glass of wine and Jenny, looking stunning as ever, broke down in tears. Lizzy was rather shocked and was not sure what to do. She was never very good in this type of situation. She did manage to stop her crying. Jenny was very unhappy. She had had enough of dating and now wanted that Mr Right, so much so, that it had upset her. Lizzy found this   whole   conversation   rather weird. This was definitely not the confident Jenny she knew. The one that always got the bloke. No this was a quivering wreck. This was the real Jenny.

It was not long and Jenny had composed herself. She shrugged of her tears as a moment of insecurity. Lizzy admitted that she also wanted that Mr Right and all women do. She was not about to cry over not having him though, that was for sure. The girls had managed to polish of the bottle before Stuart had arrived. They were now on high spirits, laughing and joking as if the incident had never taken place.

Lizzy let Stuart into the house and she introduced Jenny. Stuart's tongue dropped to the floor, not literally, but Lizzy caught his reaction to her. She was not sure what to make of it, as his eyes lingered as they shook hands. This man had told Lizzy that he was in love with her. She had believed him, and that is probably why she was seeing him. She had a man that was in love with her. That felt nice to Lizzy. She did not feel the same so never ever mentioned it. However, the reaction he had given when he had seen Jenny, made Lizzy doubt anything he had said.

Stuart and Jenny were in full conversation in the cab. Lizzy could not get a word in. She dismissed any negative thoughts. As it was later than they had expected they went straight to the night club. Stuart went to the bar and bought both girls a glass of wine. There was three parts to this club. As you entered, there was a bar and a few sofas dotted about. The music was not played at full pelt, so it was a chatting area. As Stuart and Jenny had not stopped talking Lizzy beckoned them to the sofa. To her amazement Stuart sat next to Jenny and Lizzy was shoved on the end. Needless to say, once again it was like she was banned from the conversation. Lizzy drunk her wine and ordered another. She was slowly getting sloshed and bored. She decided to go into the other room. There was a dance floor and DJ. She told Stuart where she was going and it was as if she was not even there. Fuck you then, Lizzy thought.

As she walked through the doors, there was an

abundance of people, jigging to the music. The DJ was playing some of the garage anthems and Lizzy loved it. She drunk her wine, and wiggled her arse as she mooched to the dance floor. Franky Knuckles, Tears was playing and she started to dance to the music. She was surrounded by a group of five young lads and three young women. All of them in their early 20's. She was not bothered; they were all dancing to the music and smiling at each other. The DJ was mixing in one anthem after another and she had not stopped dancing for what seemed like an eternity. One of the young men gave her a drink and the other gave her a cigarette. It was quite funny, as she had now become one of the group. They all stood by the side of the dance floor and Lizzy was chatting to one of the lads and his girlfriend. The conversation was light and they asked Lizzy why she was on her own. She explained the scenario and the girl was absolutely stunned and could not believe that Lizzy had taken everything in her stride. Lizzy did not want to think about it. She had been left on her own, but fortunately she knew how to have a good time. She could trust Jenny. Stuart allegedly loved her, so she had nothing to worry about. Lizzy dismissed the girl's negativity, but it still bothered her.

Lizzy leant over to light her cigarette and was stunned as she was grabbed from behind around the waist. She could also feel someone kissing her checks. As she spun around, she saw Stuart, all smiles with Jenny behind him.

"Come on babe, we are going now" he said.

Lizzy said her fair wells to her new found friends of the evening and left with Stuart and Jenny. She was not happy about what had happened, but continued to dismiss the thoughts. They dropped Jenny off in the cab first. Lizzy made excuses for Stuart not to come in and he headed back off to Brentwood.

The following morning Stuart called Lizzy. He sounded annoyed and Lizzy questioned his tone. "I saw you with those guys. You were all over them; who do you think you are?" he was now shouting.

"You wanna calm down mate" said Lizzy quite

sternly. "Hold up one second" she continued. "I was dancing and they were dancing. I got chatting to them and their girlfriends. You left me alone remember, all night. Too fucking busy talking to Jenny. You did not even acknowledge I was there. The only time you bothered was when you saw me chatting to the guy. But it's alright for you to do that then is it? Take me out and fuck off with me mate all fucking night long. Hypocrite, fuck off". Lizzy was fuming and she now realised just how much that this had bothered her. She was glad that he had bought it up, as she would probably not have mentioned it.

Stuart screamed back at Lizzy. "Don't start with me. You're fucking mate put it on me all night. She was the one........"

Lizzy stopped him in his tracks. "Even if that was the case, you never had to spend the whole night with her though did you? No. You could have, at any point in time, remembered that you were supposed to be out with me, and made sure that you kept your distance from her. She is my mate and she would not do that to me. So you are talking shit. Blaming her so that you don't have to take the blame" Lizzy was becoming more annoyed.

"If you don't believe me, ring her and ask her then" he said.

Lizzy slammed down the phone and promptly rung Jenny.

"Hey Jen, it's Lizzy. How are you?" Cut the small talk Lizzy thought to and get to the point.

"I have just had a row with Stuart. He told me that you flirted with him last night and that you kept coming onto him. Is this true" she questioned Jenny.

There was a silent pause from Jenny before she said "I cannot believe that you have even questioned my friendship like that".

Lizzy now felt embarrassed, but she had to know. Why would he say those things? Why would he insist that she call Jenny? Was he trying to call her bluff? Why should she have even bothered to ask Jenny the question? Surely she should not doubt her friend. Lizzy mind was now doing overtime and she made small talk with Jenny, apologised and decided to call Stuart back.

"I have spoken with Jenny and she said that she did not flirt with you. Why would you say those things?" Lizzy was now questioning Stuart. However, the damage was done and Lizzy did not know who was telling the truth. So, she dumped Stuart and had less time for Jenny. Although Jenny had denied all allegations, it never warranted why they had spent so much time together that evening, leaving Lizzy on her own. Whatever had happened, Lizzy felt betrayed and disrespected by both of them? She never went to Cyprus.

Chapter 16

It had been a while now since she had even bothered with a man. One year in fact. Stuart had continued to call her but she got rid of him. He could never be trusted again as far as Lizzy was concerned. She was glad really, as she was just making do, or killing time with him. She did not like him much at all. All the signs were there at the beginning of the relationship. Yet she had ignored them. She could kick herself for venturing into it with him. He was good fun and took her out, but that was it. Lizzy did not take any shit from guys. She had her fair share over the years and had got to the point whereby she would become unavailable at the first sign of trouble.

Looking back she was glad that she had put the ad in the paper. It had made her realise that she was not some sad old woman and it had put everything back into perspective for her. She had lost a friend because of it, but had assured herself that it would have happened anyway.

So what, if she did not have a man. She did not need one. Things were ticking along nicely just as they were. She would talk with Kai at the gym. Her fitness levels had increases dramatically and she was looking really good. Kai was a funny one and she could not make him out. They kept arranging to meet to do classes together. They never exchanged numbers. They would have coffee after the class so they could confirm their next meeting. She could see that he was interested in her. It showed in his eyes. He had made it quite clear that he did not want a commitment with any woman. Lizzy was not up for that. She had had enough of casual. However, she could see that they could indeed become good friends. That, thought Lizzy, would be very nice indeed and she was looking forward to further developing a friendship with him.

She would flirt with Luke; just to keep him interested

enough for her to have some attention.

She was spending more time with her daughter. She enjoyed that. Her daughter had passed her A Level's and was working in the city in a bank. She was proud. They would go out once a week, drinking, cinema or even to a restaurant. Lizzy knew it would not be long before she flew the nest, so she was enjoying having her around and spending every opportune moment she had.

She was not bothered about blokes. No, she was not bothered at all.

Her rampant rabbit was now her best friend, again, and she would sit and watch re-runs of friends on the cable along with Will and Grace. It was winter and she loved to curl up on the sofa with a quilt and a glass of wine with no interruptions. She hated winter but she was happy.

Life was peachy. Well for now anyway. She was just waiting for the next episode of a whirl wind romance. This time, she would get it right. True to her word, it was not long and she had met the next chapter in her long list of men and romance.

Chapter 17

His name was Jim. Not a very creative name. He was 5ft 10, very lean and toned, blue eyes and mousey brown hair. Jim was from Liverpool. It was May and spring was definitely in the air. Lizzy was happy that the sun was shining and the days and evenings were bright.

She was managing the contract at another site for the past three weeks and Jim was a contractor there. It was and imperative that the work was completed on time. She would speak with Jim daily. His accent was a turn on for Lizzy and she found him most attractive. Nearing the end of the contract Jim had asked Lizzy to go out with him on a date. At first she was a bit apprehensive. He had given her his number and she decided to call him. They had a brief chat and arranged to meet on the Friday night. They would see a movie and maybe have a drink first.

Lizzy felt different about this time. She had been quite determined not to date men. She was not ready for love, again, but thought it would be good to date. Jim was up for the deal. She had told him that she only wanted to go out on a platonic basis. He had agreed and seemed quite happy with the scenario. Lizzy should have guessed that any man would more than likely say the same given the opportunity. He was a charmer. Jim had the gift of the gab and was very amusing. Lizzy liked a man that made her laugh. Jim had made her laugh every day for the past three weeks that he was on site.

Lizzy was very nervous prior to meeting Jim. She was not sure why. After all he was only a bloke and she should be used to dating by now. But with each date she had a new experience, good and bad. They had met at the site where he had been working and she parked her car and jumped into his Audi. On the way to the cinema Jim was very chatty, as usual. He also seemed rather hyper and Lizzy was not sure why. She had started to wonder whether he was a   coke head, as he was often very hyper. As he was talking she found herself staring at his nose, looking for any signs. During the journey to the cinema she also found herself staring at his pupils to see if they were dilated. She was not too bothered either way, but after her bad incident with the pill she liked to keep away from drugs especially the class A type. She knew that cocaine was rife in the clubs and even the pubs and she had a few associates that could not go out without it. It had become the new accessory. She had dabbled, but did not care for the come down that she had experienced, so therefore had decided to leave it alone. She had also seen the transformation it had on some people, and had witnessed some of her closest friends change dramatically for the worse. In turn they were no longer her friends.

Rather than assume she left the thoughts of Jim being a coke head drift away. They arrived at the cinema early, bought the tickets and went to the wine bar next door. Lizzy still felt somewhat awkward. But after a couple of glasses of wine she relaxed. Jim told Lizzy about his family and how he ended up living in Luton. He was very attractive and she quite fancied him. It could have been the wine, but the more he chatted the more she warmed to his personality.

Jim was still hyper and declared that he did not want to see the film, even though he had bought the tickets. Lizzy suggested he get a refund and then head back to her car. She was rather disappointed as she was looking forward to watching the movie.

As they drove back there was an uneasy silence. Lizzy was rather pleased to be going home. She did not like disappointments. She thanked Jim for the date, got out of his car, got into hers and began her drive home. It was still relatively early. Lizzy was in two minds as to whether she should go home or meet up with Shelley. Before she had made up her mind she was already parking the car on the drive.

What a strange evening thought Lizzy as she curled up in bed.

Lizzy was woken by her mobile phone. It was Jim. She had slept in and this was very unusual for her. Regardless of what day it was she was normally awake by 7am. It was 10.30am.

"Hi Lizzy, I had a great time last night" said Jim.

Lizzy was puzzled.

"I'm going to Liverpool for the rest of the weekend and I would like you to come. No strings. What do ya say?" he asked.

Lizzy was now shocked. "No Strings? She wanted this clarified.

"Yep no strings" he confirmed.

"OK then, we will be coming back Monday?" she asked.

"Yep. Meet me at South Mimm's. You can leave your car there and I'll drive the rest of the way" he said.

Lizzy agreed. She got out of bed, showered and packed a weekend bag. She was now very excited. This should be fun she thought.

On the way to South Mimm's, she decided to call Jim to make sure that he would be there for when she arrived. He had booked a hotel for the two nights of which was just outside of the town centre.

Lizzy had forgotten how long the journey was to Liverpool and she was rather agitated in the car. Jim sensed her discomfort and made a few jokes to lighten her mood. It was as if he had read her mind when he stated that he was not a psycho and she could relax. Lizzy thought it weird that he even thought that, even though that was exactly what she was thinking.

Maybe this was not a good idea. She had thought. It was too late now as they pulled into the drive way leading to the hotel. The hotel had beautiful gardens surrounding it. All of the spring flowers were out in full bloom. The hotel dated back to 1800's and was in the middle of a refurb. The entrance led to a rest room area that had leather sofas and a log fire blazing.

Lizzy and Jim walked to the reception area where he ordered pink champagne.

"For the beautiful lady" he told the receptionist.

The room was tiny and had a double bed. Lizzy was a bit put out by this as she had specified on more than one occasion that she wanted a platonic affair. Jim was very apologetic and said that he would sleep on the floor. Lizzy had all angles covered as she had bought her cotton passion killer pyjamas with her.

"There's no need. I'm sure we can both sleep in the bed without having sex" she said.

Please God, she thought.

Jim smiled as he opened the champagne. This indeed was Lizzy's favourite and she was feeling very good about the fact that he had remembered and bought it. They made a toast to the weekend and Lizzy run the shower.

She took her champagne into the bathroom with her, locked the door and immersed herself under the jet of water. This was going to be fun. She finished her glass and put on her large white towelling dressing gown. Another passion killer. She was determined not to encourage him sexually in any form. As she opened the bathroom door, Jim was naked. Lizzy was not sure which way to look, but could clearly see every rippling muscle in his body. He was surely the fittest looking fella she had ever seen in the flesh. He did not seem bothered that he had nothing on and strolled over to Lizzy, filled her glass with champagne and went into the bathroom to shower. He came out with a towel wrapped around his waist and his body was glistening with the water droplets. *Wow,* Lizzy had thought, *get a load of that.*

She tried her best not to stare at him and his

114

nakedness, and made general conversation.

"I have booked a restaurant in town, Lizzy. Do you like Italian?" asked Jim.

"Yes Jim that would be lovely" said Lizzy feeling rather excited.

Lizzy was starting to get wrapped up in the romance of it all and was very glad that she had come to Liverpool with Jim. He was indeed charming, sophisticated and a gentleman. She had nothing to worry about, or so she thought.

Jim had finished using the bathroom and Lizzy went back inside, closed the door and got dressed. She blow dried her hair and applied her make up. As she opened the door, Jim was sitting on the bed staring at her.

"Lizzy, you look sensational". He was now staring at her with a wide smile. "I'll be ready in 5".

Lizzy sat on the bed drinking the champagne. She was loving every minute of this and could not believe her luck. The evening continued in the same vein. Jim being the perfect gentleman and totally adoring every part of Lizzy. The food was fantastic and they had drunk a bottle of red with their meal. It had been a long day and they both appeared to be getting tired. Jim paid the bill and they ordered a taxi.

The hotel room did not seem too appealing now to Lizzy. The evening had gone so well, she was frightened of spoiling it. She did not want to have sex, but Jim had practically charmed his way into her knickers, without the physical act. As he opened the hotel room door he leant forward and gently kissed Lizzy's lips. He was a lovely kisser and they snogged for hours. As each minute went by, he was trying to get closer and closer to having sex with Lizzy and she had stopped him in his tracks on every attempt to fondle or caress her more intimate parts. They laid on the bed together.

115

"You don't fancy me do you? You don't like me do you"? Jim had said this repeatedly throughout the evening snogging session. Lizzy had felt bad that he felt this way but also knew that it was a mental trap. She was not going to be pulled into his game. Instead she agreed with him. He knew she was lying, but on the same token, did not continue with the comments. Eventually, they both feel asleep.

The following morning, Lizzy woke to find herself alone. Jim was nowhere to be seen. She started to panic and called his mobile. Jim had left to have breakfast in the hotel dining area. He said that he did not want to wake her and that she should come down for breakfast. She was not happy that she had been left alone like that and got dressed and went to find Jim. As she entered the dining area, Jim was nowhere to be found. She decided to eat first and find him after. She called his mobile again. This time he was in the rest room area. Lizzy found him sitting on one of the sofa's reading a paper. She was not amused by this sudden turnaround in his behaviour. The previous night he had done anything to please her. Now it seemed he was doing anything to piss her off.

It was not long and Jim came back on track. They strolled on the beach behind the hotel. He held her hand and stroked her back as they walked along the sand. He held her close and told her how wonderful she was. Lizzy started to think she was in a Mills and Boon book, with her shinning knight. He was very good with the charm and had probably had lots of practise. Lizzy started to become cynical and was not going to be taken in by his warm tone and kind words. She was rather chilly and had not showered before breakfast. She told Jim that she would go back to the hotel and shower. She took the key from him and he said that he would follow later.

Lizzy was not dumb. No, Lizzy was smart. She could see where he was heading with all of this and wondered why she had even gone along with it. Don't be fooled girl. She told herself whilst in the shower. Go with the flow but don't do anything that you don't want to. All of a sudden she heard the hotel room door open. She had not locked the bathroom door and could hear a voice. She shouted out to see who it was and then Jim appeared in the bathroom. She was relieved but also astonished to see that he was naked.

"Can I join you Liz?" he asked. What the hell she thought and with that Jim was in the shower with her. They kissed passionately as they rubbed shower gel over each other's body. It was rather erotic and Lizzy could see that Jim was rather aroused.

"Lizzy, quick, quick" said Jim excitedly. Jim jumped out of the shower abruptly and pulled Lizzy by the arm.

"Quick babe, I'm ready for you look. I've been waiting all weekend to get this up. Let's not waste its" he said. Lizzy looked down and Jim had the biggest erection she had seen in a long time. "I have got to have you now before it goes away again" he declared.

Lizzy was extremely confused, amazed and so not turned on by his actions and refused to comply. As she did she saw his erection disappear, like a ball deflating?

Jim sat on the bed and Lizzy could see that he appeared to be upset. Apparently, Jim had trouble getting an erection. Something to do with some medication he was on.

Great thought Lizzy. Another one with too much baggage to deal with. She liked Jim, but she did not like him that much. She would not compromise sex. She was starting to wonder what an earth it was about scousers and poor performance. It was then that she knew not to date another one.

Chapter 18

After the long weekend with Jim, Lizzy was feeling rather deflated. She had a fantastic weekend with him. They had laughed together so hard that her belly had hurt. He had organised days and nights out. She even met his son. He was 18. She was bit put off when the son started to question whether she liked his Dad. Jim had paid for everything and any time she offered to buy a drink, he would not let her. She had had one of the best weekends with Jim that she had ever experienced. Should she compromise? She loved sex and knew from previous experiences that it had to be good. If it was not, she would soon lose interest in the man. That had happened with Chris. He was a wonderful man. He would do anything for her, but the sex was shit and his psychotic behaviour. She had told herself that it could be worked on. But it never got any better. She nearly married him. She never married him based on the fact that the sex was shit. Because it was not up to scratch she stopped sleeping with him and that's when it all went wrong. That's when he became psychotic. No, she could not compromise on that. She wanted everything and she was going to get it. She was not bothered how many frogs she had to kiss to find her prince; she was determined to have everything.

She also realised that at her age, the men she would meet would have baggage. She knew they would be divorced or have kids in tow. She was prepared for that as long as it did not interfere with her life. She had a good life. She had no baggage. Her daughter was off her hands, she had a fantastic job and she was fit and healthy for her age. She was also not short of admirers.

She still longed for her prince, but would deny this to anyone that had asked her. She would play the dating game and pretend that she was alright with it. Deep down, she was not. Deep down, she still longed for the dream she had when she was a teenager. The dream she had in the past with her daughter's father. Mum, Dad and children, happily ever after. She knew that more of her own children were not on the cards as she had been sterilised a few years ago. She did not need a father for her daughter as she was now grown up. She just wanted to have good old fashioned loving and a man to look after her. Most men she had got together with, wanted her to run a round after them. As if she did not have enough to do! She wanted a man to look after her. Chris had done. He had looked after her very well, but sexually they were crap together. It was a shame, but it was so important to her. It was her way of showing a man how she felt. It was the only way she knew, apart from cooking and cleaning. She did not want to be someone's cleaner and chef. She wanted to make love with them so sweetly that it made them feel that they had no worries in the world. To do that she had to be in love with them. It made it better if they felt the same. Surely, she thought to herself, she would find a man to be in love with. In the past she had found real love, twice. Unfortunately, something always went wrong. Perhaps she gave too much. She was definitely a giver. Her two previous loves were takers. That's where it went wrong. She had ended up exhausted, with all of the effort and not getting back what she needed to refuel. She could not help herself; it was the way she was. If she liked someone, she would give them her all. It was a natural reaction for her.

She also knew that baggage fucked up people's heads. Her head was OK. Psychologically, she could deal with all sorts and she had in the past. When it came to love she was very insecure. If she did not receive reassurance she would go to pieces. The person involved would not know about her insecurity, but somehow it must have shown through. This was the only area in her life when she became weak. She was in control of every aspect of her life, but when she was in love, she was never in control of how she felt, and would want the person to know and feel what she felt. Was she ever to find what she was looking for? Was she kidding herself? Only time would tell.

It did appear that there was a developing trend in society itself. In the 60's men went to work, women stayed at home and had the children. As she was growing up, women started to become more independent, to such an extent that they did not need a man for anything, apart from sex. She had developed her adult life on this premise, that women should be independent and successful in their own right. She had liked this aspect of the society she lived in. It had made her strong and developed her character. She did not have to rely on anyone apart from herself. However, what she had also noticed was that there appeared to be a barrage of people in their late 30's upwards that are adamant that they do not want commitment in a relationship. They have been married, divorced or hurt in the past and are scared to commit for fear of reprisals. This thought Lizzy was a shame. Everyone seemed to be out for themselves. Lizzy knew that she was living in a me me society, which lacked substance and the basics of our inherent needs. People were too busy trying to fulfil their materialistic dreams, and the simple things in their life were non-existent. They lacked love and respect, but deep down wanted it. Too scared to give, they plough all of their energies into their work and money. Lizzy was also caught up in this trap but at least she had the realisation that there was more to life than that. She was not scared to give love.

Yes she had been hurt in the past, big time, but she had not been married and that was what she wanted. If she was not married by the age of 40 she resigned herself to the fact that it would never be. This saddened Lizzy, but she had mentally prepared herself for the inevitable. She wanted someone to spend her later years with. But in the meantime it was definitely fun trying to find this someone, and she was determined to have fun, regardless of the outcome. She would still keep her integrity.

So, she continued to see Jim. They had a few dates and she stayed over at his house one Saturday evening. She had been running around all day and was tired. She drove to Luton to meet him. As she entered the house he had dinner ready. He had not cooked it but ordered it from the local Chinese take away. Lizzy did not particularly like Chinese but it went down well with the glass of chilled Chardonnay that he had poured. She was becoming fond of Jim.

On this evening, Jim appeared different to Lizzy. Perhaps it was because he was on his own turf. There were pictures of him and his ex-dotted around the living room and Lizzy wondered why he would have photos of them together. He then proceeded to tell her that he actually still lived with this woman and that she had gone away for the weekend. She was very pretty with blonde hair. He did say that they were separated and that they were in the process of selling the house. Lizzy had not seen any for sale signs outside the house and wondered whether he was trying to pull a fast one. She was tired and they went upstairs. He had his own bedroom and did not share with the ex. This put Lizzy's mind to rest. Although she had thought that it could have been a set up. Why would he sleep with Lizzy in his girlfriend's bed? Surely he could not be that much of a shit.

Lizzy could not sleep. The neighbours were having a party. They had a DJ and the music was thumping. She was becoming agitated through her tiredness. Jim pressed his body against hers and before she knew what was going on they were making mad passionate love. *This was a far cry from what happened in Liverpool* she thought. He had all of a sudden become a red-hot lover and Lizzy's body squirmed with ecstasy. Not once, but three times. No compromise needed there then!

After this incident, Jim's attitude towards Lizzy changed. He started to become demanding with her time. He wanted to see her when he wanted and there was no compromise. It all ended when Jim wanted to come and see Lizzy. She had already arranged to go out with some friends and said that he was welcome. She was not prepared to drop her arrangements. Jim finished with her that evening, on the phone. Lizzy was put out by this behaviour and could not understand what was going on. So instead of trying to find out, she deleted his numbers. Lizzy would not allow people to disrespect her. Common courtesy is all that was needed. Jim rang Lizzy a couple of times after. She tried to reconvene a relationship with him, but his attitude continued. She had been here before and was not prepared to go through it again.

This definitely was the last scouser she would get involved with, Lizzy told herself.

Lizzy did not like men who expected her to change or drop her plans, just because they want to see her. She had a lot of that when her daughter was little. Men used to think that because she was a single mum, and lived by herself, that she would be readily available at any given point in time. They all came unstuck when they realised that she was an independent woman. She was just as busy as they were, and they could never understand it. They also did not like the fact that she had a life of her own and this soon became an obstacle for them. So much so, they would not bother with her. She had learnt to deal with it and therefore not get close to just anyone. Unfortunately she got close to the wrong ones. The ones that had either hit her or tried to take advantage of her in some way.

Chapter 19

All through her life, for some unknown reason, she attracted men that were weak. Either that or they had so much baggage that they could not deal with, that it had interfered in her life. She was not prepared to get involved and she certainly was not going to sort out anyone else's problems. Yet, once again, when she was in love, she would do anything and became weak herself. This had happened with her second love.

She had known this one when she was younger. She had bumped into him in Macdonald's, of all places. She was with her daughter and he was with his Mum. She also knew his Mum. They got chatting and exchanged numbers.

He was 5ft 11, stocky and very intelligent. She fell in love with him immediately. If she could climb into his skin to get closer to him, she would have done. He had nothing to offer her at all. He did not work, wanted to be a musician, but was already 40 years of age. He had no chance in hitting the big time in that respect. But Lizzy respected him for following his dream. She was at University, her last year, and was totally skint. She had not expected him to turn up on her doorstep and declare that he had told his ex that he was in love with her and that he was now going to live with her. She let him in, even though she did not know that he had been living with someone else. She loved him with all of her heart. Why she did not know? It was all sort of unexpected, like cupid had launched his arrow straight at her heart.

She did not expect that he would take over the house. She did not expect that he would not contribute to the running of the house in any form and she did not expect that he would bring his kids around without even asking her. She also did not expect him to entertain women in her flat whilst she was away for the weekend. Something he never denied. But as she was in love, she was weak. Anything he wanted he got. She would cancel her appointments and social engagements to be with him.

He had not asked her to do so, but she did it anyway. She was totally besotted by this man. Just the thought of him made her go weak. It was as if he had taken her over. At first she did not mind. The feelings she had were wonderful.

All off her friends had told her that he was a loser. She never listened. She knew that they were right, but she never listened. She did not want to hear it and she would not accept it. This had gone on for months. Even his Mum was not happy with how he was. He started smoking weed. Constantly puffing away every hour of every day. He became paranoid and jealous of Lizzy. She was at University studying for a degree and he had nothing. In the early months of the relationship, they had so much fun together. They'd laugh and joke, party and socialise. Always at Lizzy's expense. This had bothered her, but she still continued with it.

It was the summer break prior to her final year. They had spent all of their time together. She would work in the city during the day and they would make love every night. Unbeknown to her that he was also entertaining other women whilst she was at work. She only found this out after they had split. It was a nasty separation.

This one particular occasion, Lizzy's daughter was staying at her Nan's for the weekend. Lizzy was trying to study. She was tired. She had exams due and she was determined to get through them. He was playing his music and trying to distract her. He did not want her to study and was making that quite clear, from the music pounding out of the speakers.

She was aiming for a 1st and was more than capable as her grades to date proved that it was possible. He had other ideas. Lizzy's patience run out and she asked him to turn the music off so she could study. He refused and demanded that she went the library and study there. Lizzy was fuming. How dare he fucking tell her to leave her own house? He was just a lodger, and it was at that point she realised what a looser he actually was. He had done what he set out to do. He created a row and prevented her from studying. He then had the cheek to steal her study books. In an attempt to get the books back, she agreed to go to the library. He refused to let her leave the house, blocking her way out at the living room door. He thought he was funny. He stood there with this smirk on his face, and Lizzy wanted to punch him. In fact she did. She punched him full on the nose and knocked his glasses flying. Who the hell did this man think he was? He bent down and picked up his glasses, placing them back on his face. He stood back in amazement. Shocked that she had lashed out. His manipulative ways had ceased to work and it was clear from his facial expression, including broken glasses hanging across his nose, that he didn't know what to do. He flinched as she shouted at him to get out of the way. He did, and she managed to phone the police. They arrived and removed him from the house. She was not having this man dictate to her when she was allowed to be in her own home. The home she paid for. She was not going to allow this man to ruin any prospects she had. She had struggled with her studies, yes she had been getting good grades, but she had to work hard. She had been struggling financially, with no help from him. He was not going to take away all that she had been working for. No way. That frog could truly jog on.

So, the police removed him, and she was quietly happy that he had gone. He did not return and she did not want him back. Not until she had completed her studies.

Deep down she was devastated. She had loved him so much that it had hurt. She felt like her whole world had just collapsed. She had to stay strong until after her exams and continued to focus on her work.

She had bumped into him a few months later. As soon as she saw him her heart skipped a beat. The feelings she had for him, were still deep. Yet, he did not seem bothered about it apart from having to live at his Mum's temporarily. It took Lizzy four years to get over him. He had had a deep impact on her. Even today, she has warm feelings for him. She would never return to him. He was not for her.

125

It was about two years later and he had called her house phone. She was with Chris. He, the loser ex, was having a house warming party at his new flat and wanted Lizzy to go to the party. She could not believe the cheek of the man. He had drained her financially, emotionally and nearly cost her her degree. She never thought she would or could love any one again. He was making a point, or trying to make a point. He had his own place now, and he wanted Lizzy to know. It was his way of telling her that he didn't need her anymore and that he had 'got one up on Lizzy'. Pathetic little man. Chris was the opposite of him, the loser ex, and that's what she liked about him, or so she thought.

Men, how do they heal so quickly? Perhaps he never loved her anyway. She tried to get him out of her system and had sex with one of her best mates. That was a big mistake as it made her feel cheap, yet it was bloody awesome at the time. Gosh he was good!! Alas, she no longer sees this friend as he had taken the sex night as a sign that they were now together. Of course, Lizzy had to rectify the situation sharpish, and told him so. This had happened eight years ago and she had not found another real love since. She had plenty of dates but not love for any of them.

The whole experience with this man had made Lizzy stronger still, but it also closed a small part of her heart. In a way she was also scared to give and receive love and could understand people's insecurities. She did not want to get hurt anymore. Not to that extent. At the time she wanted to curl up and die.

Nevertheless she was always prepared to take the risk for the right man. And that right man was just lurking around the corner somewhere. She was certain of that. So knew she would continue to kiss the frogs, hoping that the prince would appear. And, if this prince had half a brain, he would be looking to find and keep her.

Chapter 20

Lizzy was on the slippery slope to depression and did not even know it. The disappointment that she had, with the romances, had made her lose all trust in men completely. Yet she wanted a companion, a partner, someone she could call her own. Someone who would have her back, yet the hope of such a reality seemed to be diminishing with every relationship she endured. No-one knew her anguish. No-one knew how she had really felt. You see, Lizzy was one of the world's strong characters. Everyone, she knew would always just expect her to carry on. Behind the smiles and the laughter, and apparent confidence, there was a women that was really insecure. She masked it so well.

She had started to feel so very alone. Yes she had friends, lots of them, but they were not close to her. She stopped letting anyone get close to her. She felt coldness within her heart. It had been a gradual process, and she was unaware as to where it has stemmed from. Where it had begun.

She had started to consume even more alcohol on a daily basis. She still managed to maintain her professional conduct and her work was not affected. Her daughter was not impressed with the drinking habit and had told her to see somebody about it. Lizzy would not have any of it. Her daughter never knew the coldness that she was feeling. The loneliness she was experiencing. Even when she was surrounded with people, she felt all alone in the room.

She would often wonder why. Why was she still single, and why had her friend betrayed her so. She was independent, solvent, determined, fun. Men loved her for that. They were the very things that that attracted men to her in the first place. She had tried to talk to Sam, but Sam always had the same answer. That Lizzy was a strong independent beautiful women, and she will find her prince, she just hadn't met him yet. But what if she didn't. What if she never did find her prince? Then what? Was she doomed to live the rest of her life as a spinster? A few years prior and this would not have been an issue for Lizzy. She had often joked that if that was the case, then she would have the most fun and enjoy it. She had meant it. She wasn't fazed by the prospect. Life is too short. So why was she fazed now? She couldn't answer the question and as usual, pushed it to the back of her mind. AGAIN.

Chapter 21

It was Saturday and Gina was having a party in Southend. Lizzy was definitely going. Sam was also going and was going to drive there and back. Sam was good for that. She did not need to drink. Lizzy was once like that but she had got to the stage where she had to drink. She thought it a waste of time to go to a party or the pub and not drink at all. The funny thing was no one had noticed Lizzy's plight. She had kept it secret from her close friends and her work colleagues.

Steve was on his way over. He was a good friend of Lizzy's and they had known each other for many years. She had met him when she was 15, and she thought at that time he was the bee's knees. Steve was older than Lizzy and already 22. She found it fascinating that a big man was interested in her. However, they became friends. Steve didn't like the age difference, and although they snogged, it never went any further. So for 22 years they were good friends.

Lizzy was pissed off. She had spoken with Kai that morning at the gym. He had turned out to be the same as any other non-prospective bloke. A player and he was playing in full force. He told Lizzy everything, of which initially she had found a bit disturbing. She had liked Kai, but was so glad that they were just friends. At least she had seen him for what he was. He had gallantly told her about his conquests, one after the other. He had no real respect for women. Yet when Lizzy had first met him, he was completely different. Mind you he had just come out of an 8 year relationship. He had been playing the single game for over a year and he had perfected it to suit his own needs.

Lizzy was fed up with it all. Fed up with the seeking a partner scenario, but also fed up of feeling lonely.

She had not noticed the effects that the alcohol was having on her. People knew Lizzy to be a fun girl, so consequently no one questioned her drinking patterns. There had been an urgent job on at work and she had worked on the Saturday morning and came home to cook dinner. She was also due to work the Sunday to ensure that the order when through with no glitches. Her daughter was out with friends and she was then going to stay at her Nan's.

Steve was due over at any time, and she decided to cook both of them a roast dinner. Steve turned up on her doorstep looking very solemn. He was really down in the dumps. His marriage had collapsed and he was not taking it well. So when he arrived at Lizzy's at 4 in the afternoon with a litre bottle of Jack Daniel's, she was not surprised. Lizzie was also feeling a bit forlorn, but in true Lizzy style, once again, she masked up her feelings to take care of her friend. He needed her right now, and even if she did want to talk about her, it wasn't going to happen. Steve was in no state to give out any advice.

They cracked open the bottle and began drinking it neat with ice. They chatted, while Lizzy mainly listened to Steve's troubles. Funny, she thought to herself, he had not even told her that he got married and had a son. These are life changing moments, and she had only found some few years after the events. Now he was whinging on about how bad he had felt about the separation. It was not long and they were both pissed. They had been sitting on the kitchen floor for hours and Lizzy had then become aware of the time. Sam would be over shortly; it was already 7 o'clock. Lizzy pulled herself up from the floor and grabbed her purse.

"Come on Steve, walk with me to the shop, I want to get another bottle of Jack Daniel's to take to the party." said an already drunk Lizzy. Steve was a bit reluctant but walked with her anyway. The shop was only 5 minutes' walk away, and Lizzy knew that although they had eaten, the risk of driving was far too high. Steve was not normally worried about driving after he had a skin full at Lizzy's house. They often drank together. Normally it would be a bottle or two of wine, and the Jack Daniels was a first. Rarely after he would crash at hers, sleeping on the sofa.

On the way back from the shop Lizzy invited Steve to

the party. She also knew that she should not go either, as she had to work the following morning. She thought it might cheer him up. He was not up for it. He was one of these guys that would come to Lizzy's house, sometimes rather late, with a bottle in tow. He'd sit there drink the drink, relax for a while and then leave. She never knew when she would see him next and she often left it to him to call her. He never took her out. In the 22 years she had known him, he had taken her out once. This had bothered Lizzy over the years as she always seemed to get the worse deal from this guy. OK they were only mates, but mates for 22 years is a long time. She was always there for him, in times of trouble. But they never actually did anything or go anywhere. It was always a visit to Lizzy at her home.

Even after the separation, he had still not offered to take her anywhere, but would talk about how he had taken this women out and that woman. Lizzy wondered why he was that way with her, but tried to not let it bother her too much. Yet it did bother her, more than she would let on.

She recalled the time when she had told him to leave her alone, and not call her any more. She was venomous with her words and he did back off for a while, only to call three months later as if nothing had happened. They had arranged to go to the South of France together. Steve had actually asked her to go with him, and she was secretly very excited about it. They had talked about it for weeks. At the last minute   Lizzy booked a long weekend off from work. She also packed last minute, in fact the morning that they were going to leave. She was even happy to pay for herself, but Steve insisted that he had it covered. It was a business trip. He had told her how he was looking forward to it and spending a bit of time with Lizzy. He knew that Lizzy could have done with a break as she had been working really hard. To her disappointment, he never arrived to pick her up. He failed to contact her and she was left wondering what an earth had happened to him. She had tried to call him the day before, yet his phone was switched off. It took him over three weeks to call her with an explanation, of which was so lucid that it was ridiculous.

Somehow Lizzy forgave him. She does not know why she forgave him, but before she did she had told him what a sorry loser he was and that she was dissolving any friendship that they had, regardless of how many years it had been. Now she does not really take notice of anything he says. He tries to be a friend to Lizzy but always let her down.

Lizzy was ready and Sam had arrived. To her amazement she had the loser with her. Lizzy was smashed by the Jack Daniel's and had wrapped a bottle in a bag to take with her. She should have left it alone at this point but had continued to drink. Lizzy was on self-destruct mode and she was about to blow at any point. She drank from the bottle on the journey to the party and made polite conversation with loser man. Lizzy had taken a dislike to him immediately, but was not sure why. He was smartly dressed and spoke with a nice tone to his voice, but there was something about him and Lizzy could not put her finger on it. Sam could sense that Lizzy did not like him and turned the music up in the car. With that Lizzy rested back into the car seat and continued to drink the Jack Daniel's from the bottle.

It seemed like they were driving for hours, but eventually got to Gina's house. There were around 40 people inside and a DJ. The DJ was playing old garage tunes and there was a happy vibe in the house. After the hellos and introductions, Lizzy began drinking from the bottle again. She was now completely smashed. Normally she would never have got to that state, but things had been bothering her inside. She was not prepared to share her drink and kept hold of it all night. She wandered aimlessly from one room to another, swigging from the bottle and then found herself speaking with Sam's loser man. Then she flipped. She had told him that he was not good enough for Sam and that he should fuck off and leave her alone. She had ranted more obscenities to him when Sam interrupted, took Lizzy to one side and told her to calm down. God knows what he must have thought, but Lizzy really did not care. She had gone passed that merry stage of drinking and was now on a different level. To be honest, she was not enjoying this level, as she appeared to be getting violent. She hated violence. So she continued to drink to try and get to the next level.

Lizzy then laid into Sam, and said things that she should not have said. Lizzy had a lot of respect for Sam and this had shocked her. Sam, being the good mate she is, decided at that point that Lizzy needed to be taken home. So she did take her home and dropped her off outside her flat. She also drove away quite sharpish and Lizzy had thought that she had probably lost her best and only friend. She felt saddened. But because of the state she was in, she just shrugged it off.

Lizzy stood staring at the street door and swaying from side to side, so much so that she lost her balance and fell into the bushes. She managed to pull herself up and get to the street door where she collapsed and passed out, with the bottle of Jack Daniel's still in her hand. A few minutes passed and Lizzy came to. She had been sick on the floor and her head really hurt. She laughed to herself thinking it was funny, and then with a fleeting thought she seemed to sober up slightly as she realised that she could have choked to death on her vomit. She fumbled for the door key and literally dragged herself to bed.

Chapter 22

The following morning she was woken by the phone continuously ringing. Her head was hurting and she had no recollection of what had happened the night before. Lizzy looked at the clock and knew it must be her work place. She was due in for 8 and it was now 11.30am. She did not pick up the phone and eventually it stopped ringing.

She had felt thirsty and her head was thumping. She was still pissed and knew that there was no way she was going to work. She sat up on the side of the bed thinking trying to remember the night's events. She needed a head ache pill and walked through to the kitchen, poured a glass of water and took a pill. As she drank the water, she began to heave. She ran to the toilet and threw up, continuously for about 5 minutes. When she was sure that she was not going to heave again, she leant over the sink to wash her face. As she looked up into the mirror, she was horrified at her reflection. Her hair was matted together from the vomit. She had slept like this all night and was disgusted with herself.

As her eyes focused she could see that her eyes were red and she had dark circles under them. She looked down her face and saw bits of sick stuck to her nose and cheek. As her eyes looked at the reflection she then noticed something peculiar. She leaned into the mirror to get a better look. Then she saw it. She had lost half of her front tooth. It was missing. She blinked and refocused thinking that she may have been hallucinating. But alas, she wasn't. The tooth was gone. Well, half of it anyway. This must have happened when she had passed out by the street door. There was no blood and it must have been a clean break.

She stared at her reflection and could not believe what she had become. She was absolutely shocked that she had let this get so out of control. Why had no one noticed the state she was becoming? She started to become angry with herself. Her beautiful teeth that she was so proud of were now ruined. She looked ugly. She had never looked at herself before with such disgust. Her heart felt heavy. Heavy with disappointment, heavy with darkness, heavy with regret. Her mind started to race. She couldn't control it. Images of herself, in her mind. Beautiful images, of the beautiful confident lady she once was. What had she done!

This was Lizzy's wake up call. She had hit rock bottom; no one had noticed her slipping, apart from her daughter with the drinking. She had no real friends and the only one that she did have, she had told to fuck off. This was not the way to carry on.

Lizzy took another headache pill, drank some water, and went back to bed. As she lay there, she made a pact to herself that she would never, ever allow herself to get to this point again. She could not have gone any lower if she had tried and she was amazed that she had let herself get this low in the first place. As her eyes closed, she knew that this was indeed a turnaround point for her, she had to learn to love herself again. She cried herself to sleep with the thoughts of determining where she had gone wrong. She knew the answer to that question. She had been too busy trying to find the love of her life, without giving herself the love that she needed. Frogs and princes could take a back seat. She needed to heal her pain and she needed to find the self-love that she had lost. Knowing Lizzy, it would not take long before she bounced back to her former self of confidence and beauty. Her teeth could be fixed, all she needed to do was to fix her soul and reproduce her aura of finesse. That process would start taking place as soon as she had slept of her hangover.

Printed in Great Britain
by Amazon.co.uk, Ltd.,
Marston Gate.